THE QUEEN'S CLASSICS

CERTIFICATE BOOKS

✳

GEORGE CRABBE

Selections from his Poetry

GEORGE CRABBE

SELECTIONS
FROM HIS POETRY

Edited
with an Introduction and Notes
by

FRANK WHITEHEAD, M.A.

LECTURER IN ENGLISH AT THE
UNIVERSITY OF LONDON INSTITUTE
OF EDUCATION

Chatto and Windus
LONDON

Published by
CHATTO & WINDUS (EDUCATIONAL) LTD
42 WILLIAM IV STREET
LONDON WC2

*

CLARKE, IRWIN & CO. LTD
TORONTO

First Published 1955
Reprinted 1961, 1964

Preface

In selecting the poems for this volume I have been guided by two main considerations. In the first place, I have tried to represent Crabbe by his best work, doing full justice in particular to the later *Tales* which have been unduly neglected in those few volumes of selections which have appeared hitherto. Secondly, I have tried to bring out to the full Crabbe's mastery of the art of the short story in verse. To this end I have avoided the use of excerpts, except in the case of *The Parish Register*; apart from this the volume consists entirely of complete Letters or Tales.

Subject to the above over-riding considerations, I hope it will be found that the selection represents adequately the variety of theme, tone and intention to be found in Crabbe's poems. Since it also illustrates quite fully the varied aspects of social life which Crabbe depicted so realistically, reading the volume may incidentally serve as a helpful introduction to the social background of the period.

The volume also contains the first serious attempt to annotate Crabbe for the benefit of the twentieth-century reader.

F. W.

Contents

INTRODUCTION

i

GEORGE CRABBE was born on December 24th, 1754, at
Aldeburgh, the small town on the Suffolk coast which had
once been a busy port but was now slowly sinking into
decay. His father, after a long period of service in the
Customs as warehouse-keeper, had risen to be collector of
salt-duties, or Saltmaster. George was sent away to a small
school first at Bungay and then at Stowmarket, where he
received as much education as was necessary to fit him to
take up the profession (in those days a rather humble one)
of surgeon. At that time a seven-year apprenticeship gave
the right to set up as an apothecary or surgeon, but a
period of study in London, attending lectures and walking
the hospitals, was a desirable further qualification. Crabbe
completed his apprenticeship, but could only scrape up
enough money for a period of eight to ten months in
London, and was even then too poor to be able to follow
a regular course of instruction. Nevertheless, he returned
to Aldeburgh in 1777 and set up in practice there in a
small way. He was not very successful, and probably not
very proficient; moreover, his enthusiasm for botany
counted against him, 'for his ignorant patients, seeing him
return from his walks with handfuls of weeds, decided
that, as Dr Crabbe got his medicines in the ditches, he
could have little claim for payment'. And in any case his
heart was no longer in medicine. While he was still an
apprentice he had written great quantities of verse and
had even contrived to get some of his efforts published in
an obscure way. Now he formed the desperate resolve of
going to London to seek his fortune there as poet, and in
1780 he set out by sea with a box of clothes, a small case of
surgical instruments, and three pounds of borrowed money
in his pocket. The disappointments and distresses of the
next twelve months were scarcely surprising, but were
certainly severe; he was only enabled to hold out for so

9

long by the encouragement and financial help he received
from his future wife, Sarah Elmy, whom he had first met
when he was only eighteen. He applied to publishers in
vain, and appealed to the leading statesmen of the day for
patronage without success. Finally, just as he was near to
having to admit failure, he had the fortunate notion of
addressing a letter enclosing some of his poems to Edmund
Burke. Burke immediately recognised the young man's
talent and promise, and set about helping him in every
possible way. Crabbe was introduced to other possible
patrons, as well as to the circle of Sir Joshua Reynolds and
Dr Johnson; a publisher was found for his poem *The
Library*; and, despite the obstacle of his limited formal
education, it was made possible for him to take holy
orders. After a brief period as curate at Aldeburgh he was
found a 'place' as domestic chaplain to the Duke of
Rutland at Belvoir Castle, where he completed *The
Village* (1783). On the immediate success of this poem
Crabbe was given two small livings which enabled him to
marry at last, and he now settled down to a long period of
quiet family life in a series of country parishes in Leicestershire and Suffolk.

What is really remarkable is the prolonged silence that
followed. After the appearance of his satirical poem *The
Newspaper* in 1785, Crabbe published nothing further for
over twenty-one years. It was not that his pen was idle.
According to his son, he wrote a prodigious amount at this
time as always, but the great bulk of what he wrote he
committed to periodic bonfires in the garden. Among the
works which failed to satisfy him were at least three completed prose novels, of which we hear that on Mrs Crabbe's
'telling him frankly that she thought the effect very inferior
to that of the corresponding pieces in verse, he paused in
his reading, and, after some reflection, said, "Your remark
is just."' The result was another of his 'grand cremations'.

When he was not writing, Crabbe occupied himself in
his duties towards his parishioners (for he was a sincere
and diligent clergyman by eighteenth-century standards);

in educating his two sons (only the two eldest of his seven children survived infancy); in pursuing his studies in botany and entomology; and, above all, in reading—poetry, novels, books of travel, Latin poetry, the Greek tragedians with the aid of a Latin translation, and works in French and Italian (languages which he had taught himself to read though without bothering about their pronunciation). But despite all this busy congenial activity and despite his modestly comfortable circumstances, there was a shadow over his life which perhaps goes some way to account for that sombre strain in his poetic outlook which has led many later critics to call him a 'pessimist'. We have little information about the protracted mental illness which afflicted Crabbe's wife, but it seems to have been some form of manic-depressive disorder which first became acute after the death of her third son in 1796 and grew steadily worse until her death in 1813. Crabbe's son tells us (and we may suppose him to have softened the reality a little) that 'during the hottest months of almost every year, she was oppressed by the deepest dejection of spirits I ever witnessed in any one', while there were also intervals in which her spirits were 'a little too high'. Crabbe appears to have played at all times the rôle of an attentive and even indulgent husband and to have remained throughout devoted to the Sarah for whose hand he had waited so long; but his son found many years later a letter written from Sarah to her husband in the early years of her marriage on the margin of which the poet had written: 'Nothing can be more sincere than this, nothing more reasonable and affectionate; and yet happiness was not granted.'

In 1807 Crabbe appeared once again before the public with *The Parish Register*. The modest though favourable reception accorded to his earlier poems can hardly have prepared him for the immediate and sweeping success of this, the first of his mature works. Among the uniformly commendatory notices, the praise of Jeffrey in the *Edinburgh Review* was decisive; within two days of the appearance of Jeffrey's eulogy the whole of the first edition was sold out. With the equally successful publication of *The Borough* in 1810 and the *Tales in Verse* in 1812, Crabbe was at the height of his fame. He was universally recognised by critics, the public and fellow-authors alike as one of the leading poets of the day, and Regency society was ready to open its doors to him on terms which quite outdid the temperate welcome offered to him a quarter of a century earlier by Dr Johnson's London. For the moment, however, his wife's declining health prevented him from making use of these opportunities, though he did indulge her inclination for a brief visit to London in the autumn of 1813.

Shortly after their return to the Rectory at Muston, in Leicestershire, Mrs Crabbe died, and two days later the poet became so seriously ill that his own life was in danger for a time. After his eventual recovery he was offered the living of Trowbridge, in Wiltshire, whither he removed in 1814 and where he remained until his death in 1832. This final period of his life was marked by a striking renewal of his health and vigour. In middle age he had suffered from attacks of vertigo and digestive disorder which for many years gave 'his bodily condition the appearances of a gradual decline'. 'In those days,' wrote his son, ' "life is as tedious as a twice-told tale" was an expression not seldom in his mouth; and he once told me, he felt that he could not possibly live more than six or seven years.' But in his old age 'it seemed that he had recovered not only the enjoyment of sound health, but much of the vigour and spirit of youthful feelings'.

Crabbe now began to mix much more freely in society (even scandalising some of his parishioners by letting himself be seen occasionally 'at a concert, a ball, or even a play'), and to pay periodic visits to London or Bath, where he was lionised to a moderate extent and where he enjoyed the company of such celebrated literary figures as Samuel Rogers, Moore, Campbell and even Sir Walter Scott. To begin with, his loneliness at Trowbridge led him to form a series of semi-romantic attachments to various young ladies, one of which (conducted entirely by correspondence) even culminated in his making a proposal of marriage. The lady turned out to be engaged already and to have encouraged his attentions only with a view to turning him over to her best friend, a Miss Charlotte Ridout, who had read all his letters and was quite willing to have his affections transferred to her. For a couple of months Crabbe seems to have been half-disposed to fall in with this curious arrangement, but in the end he drew back. Then in 1816 his second son married and came to live at the Rectory at Trowbridge as curate, and the poet gave up his thoughts of remarriage, though he still kept up his intimate correspondence with some of his 'female friends'.

In other respects his life as a clergyman continued very much on the same pattern as before, except that an interest in geology replaced his earlier pursuit of natural history. He wrote as industriously as ever, and by 1819 he had a new volume ready for publication, the *Tales of the Hall*. By now his reputation stood so high that John Murray gave him £3000 for the copyright of this and of the previously published volumes. Since the publication of *Tales in Verse* in 1812, however, the Romantic poets (and particularly Byron) had begun to make their impact on the wider public, and taste in poetry had started to change. The reviewers were, on the whole, favourable to the new volume, but it did not sell, and Murray lost the greater part of his money. Nevertheless, Crabbe went on writing in much the same style as before, and at his death in 1832 he left a collection of poems in manuscript which were published in 1834 under the title of *Posthumous Tales*.

ii

During the latter part of his life Crabbe was held in remarkably high esteem by critics and reading-public alike; to quote only one instance, Jane Austen 'thoroughly enjoyed Crabbe . . . and would sometimes say, in jest, that if she ever married at all she could fancy being Mrs Crabbe'. (*Memoir of Jane Austen*, by J. E. Austen Leigh, chapter V.) After his death, however, his reputation declined rapidly, and it is no exaggeration to say that ever since he has been seriously undervalued and regrettably little read. To make matters worse, it is his best work that has been the most neglected. Thus it will be found that the account given of him in histories of English literature is often confined almost entirely to the handful of comparatively unimportant poems which he published while still a young man, the effect being to present him as merely a minor eighteenth-century poet whose main claim to fame is that he introduced a note of bitter realism into current pastoral or sentimental descriptions of village life. It is not, therefore, out of place to insist that he is in reality by no means a minor poet; he is, on the contrary, a great writer, a master of the art of short-story writing in verse whose work will stand comparison with any of the Romantics. And the natural comparison is after all with the Romantics; we need to remember that roughly nine-tenths of his poetry was in fact written during the first three decades of the nineteenth century.

At the same time all his poetry clearly has a very special relationship to the central poetic tradition of the eighteenth century, and it is this relationship which we must consider first if we are to understand and appreciate even his mature work. Perhaps it will be best to start with a few actual quotations. Here are the opening lines of *The Parish Register*:

> The year revolves, and I again explore
> The simple annals of my parish poor:
> What infant-members in my flock appear;
> What pairs I bless'd in the departed year;
> And who, of old or young, or nymphs or swains,
> Are lost to life, its pleasures and its pains.

What are the features which enable us to recognise at once

that this belongs to the Augustan tradition of Pope and Johnson? In the first place, there is the ordered regularity of the verse-form itself. From the very beginning of his career Crabbe adopted the heroic couplet as his natural and habitual mode of expression, and in this character- istically Augustan form was written all but a negligible fraction of his vast poetic output. Secondly, we cannot fail to notice a certain elaborate formality about the poet's language. The eighteenth century had held that it was necessary to keep up the dignity of serious poetic utterance by using a special diction, a system of words 'refined' (as Dr Johnson put it) 'from the grossness of domestick use'; and despite changing fashions Crabbe never wholly dis- carded this conventional and highly artificial poetic dic- tion. Thus in the *Tales* (as in our present quotation from *The Parish Register*) he still regularly refers to his young women as 'nymphs', although in the later poems terms of this kind have to rub shoulders with a great many prosaic everyday words. And if we look again at the last four lines of our quotation, we shall find that Crabbe's roundabout way of referring to births, marriages and deaths is a legacy from the same eighteenth-century concern for linguistic propriety and decorum; certain topics could only be intro- duced into poetry by means of careful periphrasis, and the periphrasis became a habit even where the ideas them- selves had none of the objectionable associations which, in a celebrated instance, had obliged the poet Grainger to cloak 'rats' under the disguise of such a phrase as 'the whisker'd vermin race'.

A third relevant feature which the reader may have noticed is Crabbe's fondness for a rhetorical balancing of words or ideas in pairs ('old or young'; 'nymphs or swains'; 'pleasures' and 'pains'); and this is even more obvious in our next quotation, the opening lines from the Tale *Arabella*:

> Of a fair town where Dr Rack was guide,
> His only daughter was the boast and pride;

Wise Arabella, yet not wise alone,
She like a bright and polish'd brilliant shone;
Her father own'd her for his prop and stay,
Able to guide, yet willing to obey;
Pleased with her learning while discourse could please,
And with her love in languor and disease.

Here the local examples of balance—'boast and pride',
'prop and stay', 'languor and disease'—are too numerous
to be overlooked; while the final couplet, with its second
line poised neatly over against the first, shows the extension of the same principle to a larger unit of meaning. In
this last couplet, indeed, the order imposed on the ideas is
so firmly embedded in the formal pattern of the verse
itself that it is scarcely possible to distinguish between the
two; and the whole effect has an unselfconscious ease and
naturalness which shows how thoroughly Crabbe had
assimilated all that he learnt from his first master, Pope.
Actually the use of antithesis in the preceding line ('Able
to guide, yet willing to obey') is even more strongly
reminiscent of Pope. The contrast which the caesura en-
forces between the two halves of the line is given further
point by the opposition of 'willing' to 'able', and 'guide' to
'obey'; yet the verbal symmetry has not been pursued
merely as an end in itself, for as we read the line in its
context we feel it to be an integral part of the developing
argument. And it is worth stressing that Crabbe was able
to use these resources (resources of a kind to which the
heroic couplet is peculiarly well adapted) in the service of
feelings and effects quite unlike anything we find in Pope.
The following, for instance, is from his description of the
ill-treatment of an apprentice by Peter Grimes:

Pinn'd, beaten, cold, pinch'd, threaten'd, and abused—
His efforts punish'd and his food refused,—
Awake tormented,—soon aroused from sleep,—
Struck if he wept, and yet compell'd to weep. . . .

For all the tightness of the formal pattern, each item in the

mounting series of antitheses makes its own relevant contribution to the grimly compassionate realism of the
narrative.

So far our analysis of the Augustan quality of Crabbe's
poetry has confined itself to features which stand out on
the surface and can easily be recognised and identified in
isolation; but it should have become apparent, even so,
that these surface characteristics proceed from a method
of composition very different from anything the Victorians
would have recognised as 'poetic'. And it is, in fact, the
underlying principle of organisation, the principle that
shapes and determines the poetic texture itself, that is in
Crabbe invariably and essentially Augustan. This must
not be taken to mean that Crabbe's poetry is lacking in
strong feeling, or even in vivid sensuous apprehension of
the external world; this is not true of Crabbe any more
than it would be true (whatever some critics may have
said) of Pope. What is meant is rather that the poet's feelings, perceptions and intuitions are at all times controlled
and ordered by his reasoning conscious mind. The effect
is one of precise measured statement, a sober judicious
marshalling of ideas and experience, in which each word,
each phrase, each element in the formal pattern can be
seen to play its due considered part. The point will become
clearer if we let our minds dwell for a moment on the
image in the second of our quotations above:

> Wise Arabella, yet not wise alone,
> She like a bright and polish'd brilliant shone. . . .

We shall find that it is not at all difficult to reason out
exactly why the comparison to 'a bright and polish'd
brilliant' is an apt one. It makes clear that Arabella's
wisdom and learning, far from being heavy or dull, has
a sparkling, scintillating quality; it adds a suggestion of
personal attractiveness; and it hints also that her accomplishments have been carefully and deliberately cultivated
('polish'd'), and that they are intended for public display.
The image may almost be said to invite us to give our

conscious attention to just these considerations; what is more, when we have done so, we feel reasonably certain that all these points of resemblance were fully present to the conscious mind of the poet himself. Now let us compare with this a fairly representative image from a Romantic poet:

> Life, like a dome of many-coloured glass,
> Stains the white radiance of Eternity,
> Until Death tramples it to fragments. . . .

This image from Shelley's *Adonais* is certainly striking and effective, and the point it makes is not difficult to grasp in a rather generalised way. But once we let our mind dwell on its details, once we start to ask questions of it, so to speak, it proves strangely elusive; it seems as though the effectiveness depends above all on a vague suggestiveness which appeals to the feelings rather than to the intellect. The mode of operation of Shelley's image is, in fact, at the opposite pole from that of Crabbe's; and the contrast between them is one which leads us to the very heart of the more general difference between the Augustan poetic mode on the one hand and the Romantic and post-Romantic modes on the other. If we are to read Crabbe's poems with the kind of attention that they ask for and deserve, we need to approach them with an awareness that, even when the subject-matter, the feeling or the vocabulary belong to the nineteenth century, the principle that guides and controls his use of words is always thoroughly Augustan. We need to remember, in fact, that the poetic sensibility we have to do with is one which (to quote from his own preface to *Tales in Verse*) appeals 'to the plain sense and sober judgment' of its readers 'rather than to their fancy and imagination'.

Crabbe's relationship to the Augustan age goes even deeper, however, than has been so far suggested. The Augustan tradition in poetry had owed its origin to a body of assumptions which were held to be obviously acceptable to all civilised reasonable human beings—assumptions concerned not merely, not even primarily, with questions of literary 'good form', but rather with such fundamental issues as the nature and purpose of the universe, and man's duties and obligations towards society and his Creator. The general tenor of these assumptions is revealed in the unquestioning deference universally paid to such terms as Sense, Reason, Truth and Nature; and these Augustan 'positives' are the common foundation which gives strength to such different literary achievements as Addison's essays and Pope's satires, Gray's *Elegy* and Dr Johnson's critic- ism. In the same way Crabbe was able to utilise the Augustan literary tradition as a living force in his poetry only because Augustanism represented for him a living presence in the realm of everyday human behaviour. His whole outlook is based on a firm belief in the character- istically eighteenth-century values of sense, judgment, balance and moderation. In religion he upholds 'the Faith that Reason finds, confirms, avows'; he suspects zeal and enthusiasm, and regards feeling by itself as an insecure foundation for Christian belief. His morality stresses par- ticularly the virtues of moderation and self-control, and he lays a considerable (but not exclusive) emphasis upon prudence and self-interest as motives for virtuous conduct, though always in a tone which takes for granted that a temperate restrained happiness is the most that man can hope for in his present existence. When he writes of Robert and Susan (in *The Parish Register*):

> Bless'd in each other, but to no excess;
> Health, quiet, comfort, form'd their happiness;
> Love all made up of torture and delight,
> Was but mere madness in this couple's sight. . . .

the sedate movement of the verse is in itself enough to tell us that the poet implicitly endorses the attitude he is describing. Even if we met the passage out of its context (where its intention is made doubly plain through its following immediately upon the account of the conse- quences to the Miller's daughter of her 'stolen moments of disturb'd delight'), we could scarcely fail to realise that 'excess' is for Crabbe almost as much a term of reproof as the even more frequently used word 'folly'.

In general, then, Crabbe shows a firm attachment to rational values which links him decisively with the eighteenth century in more than a purely literary sense. Yet he is remarkably free from the kind of limitation which this might lead us to expect. His work shows a breadth of human sympathy and imaginative understanding which reminds us that, if Augustan, he was an Augustan who lived and wrote throughout the period of the Romantic Revival; for it seems clear that some at any rate of the vitality and energy of his mature poetry comes from his readiness to expose himself to the new currents of feeling which were stirring in England at the turn of the century. Thus he has read (with enjoyment, though not with approval) the 'novels of terror' of Mrs Radcliffe and her followers; and he has submitted himself to the experience of studying the first generation of Romantic poets (apparently with some reluctance to begin with in the case of Wordsworth and Coleridge, though he admired Burns and Scott from the first). As a result he returns repeatedly to themes and topics which are essentially Romantic— dreams, madness, childhood, even ghosts—though he treats them always in a thoroughly reasonable way, seeking to understand them, explain them and bring them within the orbit of his own framework of values. This fascinated awareness of all that is irrational or inexplicable in human behaviour is one of the qualities which enable Crabbe to avoid any suggestion of easy or shallow complacency. It gives his best work a characteristic tension which is a highly individual achievement; while at times it takes forms which bring home to us the marked affinity between his outlook and that of Jane Austen, an affinity which the latter seems instinctively to have recognised. To take one example, the ironic comedy which he extracts from Arabella's capacity for self-deception must surely have made a strong appeal to the author of *Emma*. He is also capable, however, of treating human aberration with a seriousness of tone which seems to owe more to direct personal experience than to the challenging impact of the Romantic environment. Certainly the realism of his frequent portrayals of insanity suggests that the distressing circumstances of his married life played a large part in forcing him to wrestle with areas of experience which his Augustan predecessors had tended on the whole to leave out of account; while it is perhaps from this source, too, that there stems the remarkably compassionate understanding which he extends not only to the mentally deranged but to sinners as well.

Now that we have to some extent placed Crabbe's style and outlook in their historical context, we must turn our attention to the aspect of his work which, above all else, makes him a living classic—namely, his masterly skill as a writer of short stories in verse. Of this particular bent the earlier poems give scarcely a hint; they have indeed little individual distinction, and even *The Village*, undoubtedly the best as well as the most original of them, hardly deserves the prominence which it is usually given in histories of literature. In *The Parish Register* the narrative power is certainly in evidence, though still in embryonic form. The loose discursive framework is little more than a vehicle for a number of thumbnail character-sketches (usually vivid and incisive in themselves), some of which have developed, almost unnoticed, into brief illustrative anecdotes. Of these, by far the most accomplished is the story of the foundling boy who became Sir Richard Monday; in length and scope as well as in its economy and its neatly rounded satiric point, it bears an unmistakable relation to Pope's story of Sir Balaam (in Epistle III *Of the Use of Riches*), though it has in it also a touch of the warmer sympathy of feeling which was to make the form capable of extension and development. It was in fact in his next poem, *The Borough*, that Crabbe first lighted on the genre that proved to be so ideally suited to his genius. Most of the earlier Letters consist of a description of one aspect of the life of the Borough, capped by an anecdote which illustrates and underlines the argument; in the later Letters the anecdote grows in length and importance, until finally in the Letters dealing with 'the Inhabitants of the Almshouses' and 'the Poor of the Borough' the Tale bursts out of its chrysalis and takes over entirely. Such tales as *The Parish Clerk* or *Peter Grimes* are still confined to the demonstration of a single moral theme, but in their extended narrative development, scope for characterisation, and use of dialogue they are essentially the same art-form which Crabbe was to use for the rest of his life.

The form which Crabbe has thus created for himself is a personal and extremely original achievement, yet it retains a number of features which link it very closely with eighteenth-century literary traditions. For one thing, it is unswervingly didactic. 'The end of writing is to instruct; the end of poetry is to instruct by pleasing.' Clearly it can never have occurred to Crabbe to question the validity of this dictum of Dr Johnson's. He writes always in the spirit of his own lines from *The Parish Register*:

> And could I well th' instructive truth convey,
> 'Twould warn the giddy and awake the gay.

and his footnote at the end of the tale *Arabella*, for instance, shows that he took his moral responsibilities seriously. Nevertheless, the word 'didactic' could easily convey a false impression. As we read his mature work it becomes increasingly clear that there was and could be for Crabbe no conflict, no division even, between the claims of art and of moral instruction. Secure in his conviction that the 'Nature' to which art is required to be faithful is itself the supreme repository of moral law, he can feel no temptation to distort the facts as he sees them; the 'truth' is itself bound to be 'instructive'. Thus the difference between those tales (such as *The Parish Clerk*) from which we carry away a single explicit moral lesson and those (such as *The Frank Courtship* or *Advice*) which leave behind a less easily summarised impression is merely the difference between the less and the more complex. And in his best work (and particularly in the Tales of the 1812 volume) Crabbe is increasingly preoccupied with defining the subtlety of the moral issues involved. He combines within the individual tale a richer profusion of subsidiary themes and incidents; and the overall moral purpose which unifies and controls this wealth of detail, besides being more complicated, is often implied rather than openly stated. In all of his work, however, there is only one tale (the posthumous *Silford Hall*) from which explicit moral purpose is entirely absent, and even in this case there is preserved an earlier draft in which a moral lesson is tacked on at the end.

Following closely from his moral preoccupations there is one aspect of Crabbe's characterisation which is especially noteworthy. In general, the assumption that literature should teach useful lessons which are widely applicable led eighteenth-century writers and critics to prefer those characters and situations which could be seen to be 'general' rather than 'particular'. Thus, Dr Johnson held that: 'Nothing can please many and please long, but just representations of general nature'; and what he meant by 'general' here is made plain by his further comment that whereas 'in the writings of other poets a character is too often an individual', in those of Shakespeare (whom he found pre-eminent in this respect) 'it is commonly a species'. Now Crabbe's characters are certainly not 'types' in any derogatory sense; in fact, they are likely to strike us at first as highly detailed, particularised and individual. Nevertheless, there can be no doubt that they are at the same time quite deliberately representative on two levels. In the first place, they are socially typical. Arabella's accomplishments are those of the typical bluestocking of the period. The 'Squire in *Advice* combines in his own person all the traits most commonly to be found in members of his particular social class. In fact, this tale *Advice*, taken as a whole, epitomises in a quite remarkable way a whole chapter of English social history. All the salient aspects are there, and each is given its due weight—the manners, morals and outlook of the eighteenth-century squire, the relationship between the Church and the aristocracy, the impact of the Evangelical movement, even the eventual outcome of the conflict. It is, no doubt, a perception of this quality in Crabbe that has led the social historians to take more interest in his work than most literary critics have done.[1] But over and above this, Crabbe's characters are also representative on a second and more fundamental level. They typify permanent traits in human nature, so that the moral issues and conflicts which they embody have a universal and timeless significance. Thus, in the case of *Advice*, we can readily think of parallels in the modern world to the dilemma of the young priest, caught between his devotion to his ideals and his preference for a comfortable life untroubled by conflict with the powers that be, yet sufficiently sensitive to be made uncomfortable in the event by the excesses of some of his own party. Perhaps in our modern parallel the ideals which caused the conflict might not be specifically religious in character, but in any case it is evident that the theme and its treatment has a relevance which is not confined to the particular historical period depicted. Yet, for all their representative significance on these two levels, we never doubt, while reading, that the squire and the priest are each individual sentient human beings. In its own lesser way Crabbe's achievement in this respect is comparable in kind with that of Chaucer in the *Canterbury Tales*; for in Crabbe's tales also we shall find (to borrow the words of Mr John Speirs in his *Chaucer the Maker*) 'the kind of characterisation which distinguishes the English novel from Bunyan to Henry James—characters which, while exquisitely realistic in detail, are morally and socially typical'.

One further aspect of Crabbe's art must be touched on briefly—the extraordinary frankness and comprehensive-

---

[1] See, for instance, the Hammonds' tribute in *The Village Labourer*: '... Crabbe, to whose sincere and realist pen we owe much of our knowledge of the social life of the time.'

ness of his portrayal of the England of his day. He is not at all inhibited by moral squeamishness or literary decorum; there is practically no topic which he avoids, and no level of rural life to which he does not somewhere bring the same complete assurance of touch. At the same time, the generous range and sweep of his art is something more far-reaching than any discussion in terms merely of subject-matter could suggest. It can be seen above all in the remarkable variety of emotions, themes and artistic purposes to which the Tale lends itself in his hands. This variety cannot be adequately represented in a limited selection, though some idea of its scope may be gained by placing, for instance, *Procrastination* alongside *The Wager*, and then noticing the distance which separates *The Frank Courtship* from either.

The Frank Courtship, in fact, can conveniently be discussed at greater length, since it offers the best possible example of the complex yet closely unified structure which Crabbe is capable of achieving within the individual tale. The events themselves are straightforward enough. A well-to-do merchant belonging to an austere dissenting sect allows his daughter Sybil to be brought up by a widowed aunt whose way of life is more frivolous and worldly. The girl acquires tastes and views which at first are concealed from the father, but which come out into the open when he plans to marry her to an eligible but sober-minded young dissenter. Shocked by the independence of her outlook, he tries to threaten or cajole her into submission, but she remains stubbornly determined to exercise her own judgment in regard to the suitor whom she has not yet seen. When finally an interview is arranged between the two young people, each approaches it with misgiving and suspicion, and they spend their time shrewdly pointing out each other's faults and weaknesses. Nevertheless, the tale ends with the certainty that the marriage will take place after all in a spirit of mutual compromise. But this bald summary gives no indication of the rich pattern of vividly observed detail that makes up the real interest of Crabbe's ironic social comedy. The complexity of this pattern is, as so often in Crabbe, a matter of holding a just balance between conflicting attitudes and values each of which has something to be said for it. The conflict is even observable within Sybil herself, for she is a character 'in the round', recognisably her father's daughter as well as the protégée of her more worldly aunt; the way her delightful vivacity verges at times on impudence is admirably rendered in her pert exchanges with her parents and with Josiah, yet at the same time we are convinced of the 'secret bias to the right' which gives her qualms of conscience over her deception of her father. But this is only one instance of the more general juxtaposition of Puritan and worldly values which is so arranged as to throw into relief the faults and limitations of each side. Thus in their final encounter we are compelled to recognise the element of justice in Josiah's denunciation of Sybil's vanity, as well as in her attack upon his 'formal ways'; it is in keeping with the spirit of the poem that their interview should end as a drawn battle. This main theme is supported by several lesser but related themes. A balance has also to be struck, for instance, between Sybil's insistence upon being loved—

> 'I must be loved', said Sybil, 'I must see
> The man in terrors who aspires to me.'

—and her mother's recommendation of a sober prudent union based upon 'esteem' and aiming only at domestic peace. But we have room for only one illustration of the economy with which Crabbe ensures that every detail he records has a relevance to the artistic purpose of his tale as a whole.

Consider, then, the description of the Kindred's household near the beginning of the poem (lines 41-78). Just as Crabbe's rightly praised descriptions of natural scenery are so often there not simply for their own sake but as vital contribution to the tone and atmosphere of the poem in which they occur; so too in this case his superbly detailed and meticulous realism has a definite rôle to play

It carefully defines for us the complacent conviction of their own worth which lies behind the austere manners of the 'saints'; and by way of the treasured portrait of the Protector Cromwell ('Forced, though it grieved his soul to rule alone') it brings out the connection between this attitude of self-satisfied righteousness, and the father's overbearing domestic tyranny, the same tyranny which is later to show itself comically baffled by Sybil's unlooked-for defiance. Furthermore, the insight thus established into the motive force behind Puritan austerity lends deeper point to Sybil's perception, later on, that in Josiah's plain and formal attire there is

'something of the pride
That indicates the wealth it seems to hide.'

Only in the course of reading the tale as a whole, however, would it be possible to demonstrate at all fully the way in which the local wit and point continually reach out, both backwards and forwards, with the effect of a sort of ironic counterpointing, to every corner of the poem. All that has been attempted here is to suggest the kind of intricate interlocking which we find, in Crabbe's best tales, between the parts and the whole; and to stress that more than a single reading is needed if we are really to appreciate this complexity of structure. This does not, of course, mean that the tales cannot be read straight off as admirable and absorbing pieces of storytelling; it does mean that the more prolonged and attentive our acquaintance with them becomes, the better placed we shall be to understand his contemporaries' high estimate of Crabbe and to enjoy the qualities which entitle him to a place among the great poets of the English tradition.

iii

In the present volume the text of the posthumous tale *Silford Hall* has been taken from the 1834 edition of the poet's works. The text of all the remaining poems has been taken from the 1823 edition, the last edition published during the poet's lifetime. There were, in fact, two substantially identical editions published in 1823, one in five volumes and the other in eight volumes. In general, the text followed in the present edition is that of the eight-volume version, but in one or two very minor instances where readings differ, that of the five-volume version has been preferred. Care has been taken to retain Crabbe's own punctuation throughout, despite its occasional illogicalities. In the case of *Silford Hall* a few obvious mistakes in the punctuation of the 1834 edition have been corrected; but it has seemed best to leave the use of Capital letters unchanged, even though it may be suspected that certain apparent inconsistencies in this respect would have been removed had the poet been alive to see the tale through the press.

The notes at the end of the volume attempt to do two things: first, to supply the background information necessary for a full understanding of the poet's intention; and second, to provide questions and comments helpful to the appreciation of the poems as literature. Where they are concerned with local qualities, these critical 'pointers' come at the appropriate place in the general body of notes; but there will also be found at the end of the notes on each poem at least one question of a kind which should enable the reader to work out for himself the poetic intention of the poem as a whole—and ultimately (it is hoped) to make his own critical assessment of it.

From *The Parish Register* (1807)

PART I. BAPTISMS

The Child of the Miller's Daughter, and Relation of her Misfortune—A frugal Couple: their Kind of Frugality—Plea of the Mother of a natural Child: her Churching—Large Family of Gerald Ablett: his Apprehensions: Comparison between his State and that of the wealthy Farmer his Master: his Consolation—An old Man's Anxiety for an Heir: the Jealousy of another on having many—Characters of the Grocer Dawkins and his Friend: their different kinds of Disappointment—Three Infants named—An Orphan Girl and Village Schoolmistress—Gardener's Child: Pedantry and Conceit of the Father: his Botanical Discourse: Method of fixing the Embryo-fruit of Cucumbers—Absurd Effects of Rustic Vanity: observed in the Names of their Children—Relation of the Vestry Debate on a Foundling: Sir Richard Monday—Children of various Inhabitants—The poor Farmer—Children of a Profligate: his Character and Fate—Conclusion.

THE year revolves, and I again explore
The simple annals of my parish poor;
What infant-members in my flock appear,
What pairs I bless'd in the departed year;
And who, of old or young, or nymphs or swains,
Are lost to life, its pleasures and its pains.
  No Muse I ask, before my view to bring
The humble actions of the swains I sing.—
How pass'd the youthful, how the old their days;
Who sank in sloth, and who aspired to praise;   10
Their tempers, manners, morals, customs, arts,
What parts they had, and how they 'mploy'd their parts;
By what elated, soothed, seduced, depress'd,
Full well I know—these records give the rest.

————

  WITH evil omen we that year begin:
A Child of Shame,—stern Justice adds, of Sin,
Is first recorded;—I would hide the deed,
But vain the wish; I sigh and I proceed:
And could I well th' instructive truth convey,

'Twould warn the giddy and awake the gay.   20
  Of all the nymphs who gave our village grace,
The Miller's daughter had the fairest face:
Proud was the Miller; money was his pride;
He rode to market, as our farmers ride,
And 'twas his boast, inspired by spirits, there,
His favourite Lucy should be rich as fair;
But she must meek and still obedient prove,
And not presume, without his leave, to love.
  A youthful Sailor heard him;—'Ha!' quoth he,
'This Miller's maiden is a prize for me;   30
Her charms I love, his riches I desire,
And all his threats but fan the kindling fire;
My ebbing purse no more the foe shall fill,
But Love's kind act and Lucy at the mill.'
  Thus thought the youth, and soon the chase began,
Stretch'd all his sail, nor thought of pause or plan:
His trusty staff in his bold hand he took,
Like him and like his frigate, heart of oak;
Fresh were his features, his attire was new;
Clean was his linen, and his jacket blue: 40
Of finest jean, his trowsers, tight and trim,
Brush'd the large buckle at the silver rim.
  He soon arrived, he traced the village-green,
There saw the maid, and was with pleasure seen;
Then talk'd of love, till Lucy's yielding heart
Confess'd 'twas painful, though 'twas right to part.
  'For ah! my father has a haughty soul;
Whom best he loves, he loves but to control;
Me to some churl in bargain he'll consign,
And make some tyrant of the parish mine: 50
Cold is his heart, and he with looks severe
Has often forced but never shed the tear;
Save, when my mother died, some drops express'd
A kind of sorrow for a wife at rest:—
To me a master's stern regard is shown,
I'm like his steed, prized highly as his own;
Stroked but corrected, threaten'd when supplied,

His slave and boast, his victim and his pride.'
    'Cheer up, my lass! I'll to thy father go,
The Miller cannot be the Sailor's foe;   60
Both live by Heaven's free gale, that plays aloud
In the stretch'd canvas and the piping shroud;
The rush of winds, the flapping sails above,
And rattling planks within, are sounds *we* love;
Calms are our dread; when tempests plough the deep,
We take a reef, and to the rocking sleep.'
    'Ha!' quoth the Miller, moved at speech so rash,
'Art thou like me? then where thy notes and cash?
Away to Wapping, and a wife command,
With all thy wealth, a guinea, in thine hand;   70
There with thy messmates quaff the muddy cheer,
And leave my Lucy for thy betters here.'
    'Revenge! revenge!' the angry lover cried,
Then sought the nymph, and 'Be thou now my bride.'
Bride had she been, but they no priest could move
To bind in law, the couple bound by love.
    What sought these lovers then by day, by night?
But stolen moments of disturb'd delight;
Soft trembling tumults, terrors dearly prized,
Transports that pain'd, and joys that agonized: 80
Till the fond damsel, pleased with lad so trim,
Awed by her parent, and enticed by him,
Her lovely form from savage power to save,
Gave—not her hand—but ALL she could, she gave.
    Then came the day of shame, the grievous night,
The varying look, the wandering appetite;
The joy assumed, while sorrow dimm'd the eyes,
The forced sad smile, that follow'd sudden sighs;
And every art, long used, but used in vain,
To hide thy progress, Nature, and thy pain.   90
    Too eager caution shows some danger's near,
The bully's bluster proves the coward's fear;
His sober step the drunkard vainly tries,
And nymphs expose the failings they disguise.
    First, whispering gossips were in parties seen;

Then louder Scandal walk'd the village-green;
Next babbling Folly told the growing ill,
And busy Malice dropp'd it at the mill.
    'Go! to thy curse and mine,' the Father said,
'Strife and confusion stalk around thy bed;   100
Want and a wailing brat thy portion be,
Plague to thy fondness, as thy fault to me;—
Where skulks the villain?'——
                                    —'On the ocean wide
My William seeks a portion for his bride.'—
    'Vain be his search! but, till the traitor come,
The higgler's cottage be thy future home;
There with his ancient shrew and care abide,
And hide thy head,—thy shame thou canst not hide.'
    Day after day was pass'd in pains and grief;
Week follow'd week,—and still was no relief: 110
Her boy was born—no lads nor lasses came
To grace the rite or give the child a name;
Nor grave conceited nurse, of office proud,
Bore the young Christian roaring through the crowd:
In a small chamber was my office done,
Where blinks through paper'd panes the setting sun;
Where noisy sparrows, perch'd on penthouse near,
Chirp tuneless joy, and mock the frequent tear;
Bats on their webby wings in darkness move,
And feebly shriek their melancholy love.   120
    No Sailor came; the months in terror fled!
Then news arrived—He fought, and he was DEAD!
    At the lone cottage Lucy lives, and still
Walks for her weekly pittance to the mill;
A mean seraglio there her father keeps,
Whose mirth insults her, as she stands and weeps;
And sees the plenty, while compell'd to stay,
Her father's pride, become his harlot's prey.
    Throughout the lanes she glides, at evening's close,
And softly lulls her infant to repose;   130
Then sits and gazes, but with viewless look,
As gilds the moon the rippling of the brook;

And sings her vespers, but in voice so low,
She hears their murmurs as the waters flow:
And she too murmurs, and begins to find
The solemn wanderings of a wounded mind:
Visions of terror, views of wo succeed,
The mind's impatience, to the body's need;
By turns to that, by turns to this a prey,
She knows what reason yields, and dreads what madness
    may.   140

   Next, with their boy, a decent couple came,
And call'd him Robert, 'twas his father's name;
Three girls preceded, all by time endear'd,
And future births were neither hoped nor fear'd:
Bless'd in each other, but to no excess;
Health, quiet, comfort, form'd their happiness;
Love all made up of torture and delight,
Was but mere madness in this couple's sight:
Susan could think, though not without a sigh,
If she were gone, who should her place supply;   150
And Robert, half in earnest, half in jest,
Talk of her spouse when he should be at rest:
Yet strange would either think it to be told,
Their love was cooling or their hearts were cold.
Few were their acres,—but, with these content,
They were, each pay-day, ready with their rent:
And few their wishes—what their farm denied,
The neighbouring town, at trifling cost, supplied.
If at the draper's window Susan cast
A longing look, as with her goods she pass'd,   160
And, with the produce of the wheel and churn,
Bought her a Sunday-robe on her return;
True to her maxim, she would take no rest,
Till care repaid that portion to the chest:
Or if, when loitering at the Whitsun-fair,
Her Robert spent some idle shillings there;
Up at the barn, before the break of day,
He made his labour for th' indulgence pay:
Thus both—that waste itself might work in vain—

Wrought double tides, and all was well again.   170
　Yet, though so prudent, there were times of joy,
(The day they wed, the christening of the boy,)
When to the wealthier farmers there was shown
Welcome unfeign'd, and plenty like their own;
For Susan served the great, and had some pride
Among our topmost people to preside:
Yet in that plenty, in that welcome free,
There was the guiding nice frugality,
That, in the festal as the frugal day,
Has, in a different mode, a sovereign sway;   180
As tides the same attractive influence know,
In the least ebb and in their proudest flow;
The wise frugality, that does not give
A life to saving, but that saves to live;
Sparing, not pinching, mindful though not mean,
O'er all presiding, yet in nothing seen.
　Recorded next a babe of love I trace!
Of many loves, the mother's fresh disgrace.—
　'Again, thou harlot! could not all thy pain,
All my reproof, thy wanton thoughts restrain?'   190
　'Alas! your reverence, wanton thoughts, I grant,
Were once my motive, now the thoughts of want;
Women, like me, as ducks in a decoy,
Swim down a stream, and seem to swim in joy;
Your sex pursue us, and our own disdain;
Return is dreadful, and escape is vain.
Would men forsake us, and would women strive
To help the fall'n, their virtue might revive.'
　For rite of churching soon she made her way,
In dread of scandal, should she miss the day:—   200
Two matrons came! with them she humbly knelt,
Their action copied and their comforts felt,
From that great pain and peril to be free,
Though still in peril of that pain to be;
Alas! what numbers, like this amorous dame,
Are quick to censure, but are dead to shame!
　Twin-infants then appear; a girl, a boy,

34

Th' o'erflowing cup of Gerard Ablett's joy:
One had I named in every year that pass'd
Since Gerard wed! and twins behold at last!　　　210
Well pleased, the bridegroom smiled to hear—'A vine
Fruitful and spreading round the walls be thine,
And branch-like be thine offspring!'—Gerard then
Look'd joyful love, and softly said, 'Amen.'
Now of that vine he'd have no more increase,
Those playful branches now disturb his peace:
Them he beholds around his table spread,
But finds, the more the branch, the less the bread;
And while they run his humble walls about,
They keep the sunshine of good-humour out.　　　220
　　Cease, man, to grieve! thy master's lot survey,
Whom wife and children, thou and thine obey;
A farmer proud, beyond a farmer's pride,
Of all around the envy or the guide;
Who trots to market on a steed so fine,
That when I meet him, I'm ashamed of mine;
Whose board is high up-heap'd with generous fare,
Which five stout sons and three tall daughters share:
Cease, man, to grieve, and listen to his care.
　　A few years fled, and all thy boys shall be　　　230
Lords of a cot, and labourers like thee:
Thy girls unportion'd neighb'ring youths shall lead
Brides from my church, and thenceforth thou are freed:
But then thy master shall of cares complain,
Care after care, a long connected train;
His sons for farms shall ask a large supply,
For farmers' sons each gentle miss shall sigh;
Thy mistress, reasoning well of life's decay,
Shall ask a chaise, and hardly brook delay;
The smart young cornet who, with so much grace,　　　240
Rode in the ranks and betted at the race,
While the vex'd parent rails at deed so rash,
Shall d—n his luck, and stretch his hand for cash.
Sad troubles, Gerard! now pertain to thee,
When thy rich master seems from trouble free;

But 'tis one fate at different times assign'd,
And thou shalt lose the cares that he must find.

   'Ah!' quoth our village Grocer, rich and old,
'Would I might one such cause for care behold!'
To whom his Friend, 'Mine greater bliss would be,   250
Would Heav'n take those my spouse assigns to me.'

   Aged were both, that Dawkins, Ditchem this,
Who much of marriage thought, and much amiss;
Both would delay, the one, till—riches gain'd,
The son he wish'd might be to honour train'd;
His Friend—lest fierce intruding heirs should come,
To waste his hoard and vex his quiet home.

   Dawkins, a dealer once, on burthen'd back
Bore his whole substance in a pedlar's pack;
To dames discreet, the duties yet unpaid,   260
His stores of lace and hyson he convey'd:
When thus enrich'd, he chose at home to stop,
And fleece his neighbours in a new-built shop;
Then woo'd a spinster blithe, and hoped, when wed,
For love's fair favours and a fruitful bed.

   Not so his Friend;—on widow fair and staid
He fix'd his eye, but he was much afraid;
Yet woo'd; while she his hair of silver hue
Demurely noticed, and her eye withdrew:
Doubtful he paused—'Ah! were I sure,' he cried,   270
'No craving children would my gains divide;
Fair as she is, I would my widow take,
And live more largely for my partner's sake.'

   With such their views some thoughtful years they pass'd,
And hoping, dreading, they were bound at last.
And what their fate? Observe them as they go,
Comparing fear with fear and wo with wo.
'Humphrey!' said Dawkins, 'envy in my breast
Sickens to see thee in thy children bless'd;
They are thy joys, while I go grieving home   280
To a sad spouse, and our eternal gloom:
We look despondency; no infant near,
To bless the eye or win the parent's ear;

Our sudden heats and quarrels to allay,
And soothe the petty sufferings of the day:
Alike our want, yet both the want reprove;
Where are, I cry, these pledges of our love?
When she, like Jacob's wife, makes fierce reply,
Yet fond—Oh! give me children, or I die:
And I return—still childless doom'd to live,   290
Like the vex'd patriarch—Are they mine to give?
Ah! much I envy thee thy boys, who ride
On poplar branch, and canter at thy side;
And girls, whose cheeks thy chin's fierce fondness know
And with fresh beauty at the contact glow.'
   'Oh! simple friend,' said Ditchem, 'would'st thou gain
A father's pleasure by a husband's pain?
Alas! what pleasure—when some vig'rous boy
Should swell thy pride, some rosy girl thy joy;
Is it to doubt who grafted this sweet flower,   300
Or whence arose that spirit and that power?
   Four years I've wed; not one has pass'd in vain:
Behold the fifth! behold, a babe again!
My wife's gay friends th' unwelcome imp admire,
And fill the room with gratulation dire:
While I in silence sate, revolving all
That influence ancient men, or that befall;
A gay pert guest—Heav'n knows his business—came;
A glorious boy, he cried, and what the name?
Angry I growl'd,—My spirit cease to tease,   310
Name it yourselves,—Cain, Judas, if you please;
His father's give him,—should you that explore,
The devil's or yours:—I said, and sought the door.
My tender partner not a word or sigh
Gives to my wrath, nor to my speech reply;
But takes her comforts, triumphs in my pain,
And looks undaunted for a birth again.'
   Heirs thus denied afflict the pining heart,
And thus afforded, jealous pangs impart;
Let, therefore, none avoid, and none demand   320
These arrows number'd for the giant's hand.

Then with their infants three, the parents came,
And each assign'd—'twas all they had—a name;
Names of no mark or price; of them not one
Shall court our view on the sepulchral stone,
Or stop the clerk, th' engraven scrolls to spell,
Or keep the sexton from the sermon bell.

An orphan-girl succeeds: ere she was born
Her father died, her mother on that morn:
The pious mistress of the school sustains   330
Her parents' part, nor their affection feigns,
But pitying feels: with due respect and joy,
I trace the matron at her loved employ;
What time the striplings, wearied e'en with play,
Part at the closing of the summer's day,
And each by different path returns the well-known way—
Then I behold her at her cottage-door,
Frugal of light;—her Bible laid before,
When on her double duty she proceeds,
Of time as frugal—knitting as she reads: 340
Her idle neighbours, who approach to tell
Some trifling tale, her serious looks compel
To hear reluctant,—while the lads who pass,
In pure respect, walk silent on the grass:
Then sinks the day, but not to rest she goes,
Till solemn prayers the daily duties close.

But I digress, and lo! an infant train
Appear, and call me to my task again.
'Why Lonicera wilt thou name thy child?'
I ask'd the Gardener's wife, in accents mild: 350
'We have a right,' replied the sturdy dame;—
And Lonicera was the infant's name.
If next a son shall yield our Gardener joy,
Then Hyacinthus shall be that fair boy;
And if a girl, they will at length agree,
That Belladonna that fair maid shall be.

High-sounding words our worthy Gardener gets,
And at his club to wondering swains repeats;
He then of Rhus and Rhododendron speaks,

And Allium calls his onions and his leeks;   360
Nor weeds are now, for whence arose the weed,
Scarce plants, fair herbs, and curious flowers proceed;
Where Cuckoo-pints and Dandelions sprung,
(Gross names had they our plainer sires among,)
There Arums, there Leontodons we view,
And Artemisia grows, where Wormwood grew.
  But though no weed exists his garden round,
From Rumex strong our Gardener frees his ground,
Takes soft Senicio from the yielding land,
And grasps the arm'd Urtica in his hand.   370
  Not Darwin's self had more delight to sing
Of floral courtship, in th' awaken'd Spring,
Than Peter Pratt, who simpering loves to tell
How rise the Stamens, as the Pistils swell;
How bend and curl the moist-top to the spouse,
And give and take the vegetable vows;
How those esteem'd of old but tips and chives,
Are tender husbands and obedient wives;
Who live and love within the sacred bower,—
That bridal bed, the vulgar term a flower.   380
  Hear Peter proudly, to some humble friend,
A wondrous secret, in his science, lend:—
'Would you advance the nuptial hour, and bring
The fruit of Autumn with the flowers of Spring;
View that light frame where Cucumis lies spread,
And trace the husbands in their golden bed,
Three powder'd Anthers;—then no more delay,
But to the Stigma's tip their dust convey;
Then by thyself, from prying glance secure,
Twirl the full tip and make your purpose sure;   390
A long-abiding race the deed shall pay,
Nor one unbless'd abortion pine away.'
  T' admire their friend's discourse our swains agree,
And call it science and philosophy.
  'Tis good, 'tis pleasant, through th' advancing year,
To see unnumber'd growing forms appear;
What leafy-life from Earth's broad bosom rise!

What insect-myriads seek the summer skies!
What scaly tribes in every streamlet move!
What plumy people sing in every grove!   400
All with the year awaked to life, delight, and love.
Then names are good; for how, without their aid,
Is knowledge, gain'd by man, to man convey'd?
But from that source shall all our pleasures flow?
Shall all our knowledge be those names to know?
Then he, with memory bless'd, shall bear away
The palm from Grew, and Middleton, and Ray:
No! let us rather seek, in grove and field,
What food for wonder, what for use they yield;
Some just remark, from Nature's people bring,   410
And some new source of homage for her King.
    Pride lives with all; strange names our rustics give
To helpless infants, that their own may live;
Pleased to be known, they'll some attention claim,
And find some by-way to the house of fame.
    The straightest furrow lifts the ploughman's art,
The hat he gain'd has warmth for head and heart;
The bowl that beats the greater number down
Of tottering nine-pins, gives to fame the clown;
Or, foil'd in these, he opes his ample jaws,   420
And lets a frog leap down, to gain applause;
Or grins for hours, or tipples for a week,
Or challenges a well-pinch'd pig to squeak:
Some idle deed, some child's preposterous name,
Shall make him known, and give his folly fame.
    To name an infant meet our village-sires,
Assembled all, as such events requires;
Frequent and full, the rural sages sate,
And speakers many urged the long debate,—
Some harden'd knaves, who roved the country round,   430
Had left a babe within the parish-bound.—
First, of the fact they question'd—'Was it true?'
The child was brought—'What then remain'd to do?
Was't dead or living?' This was fairly proved,—
'Twas pinched, it roar'd, and every doubt removed.

Then by what name th' unwelcome guest to call
Was long a question, and it posed them all;
For he who lent it to a babe unknown,
Censorious men might take it for his own:
They look'd about, they gravely spoke to all,   440
And not one Richard answer'd to the call.
Next they inquired the day, when, passing by,
Th' unlucky peasant heard the stranger's cry:
This known,—how food and raiment they might give,
Was next debated—for the rogue would live;
At last, with all their words and work content,
Back to their homes the prudent vestry went,
And Richard Monday to the workhouse sent.
There was he pinch'd and pitied, thump'd and fed,
And duly took his beatings and his bread;   450
Patient in all control, in all abuse,
He found contempt and kicking have their use:
Sad, silent, supple; bending to the blow,
A slave of slaves, the lowest of the low;
His pliant soul gave way to all things base,
He knew no shame, he dreaded no disgrace.
It seem'd, so well his passions he suppress'd,
No feeling stirr'd his ever-torpid breast;
Him might the meanest pauper bruise and cheat,
He was a footstool for the beggar's feet;   460
His were the legs that ran at all commands;
They used on all occasions Richard's hands:
His very soul was not his own; he stole
As others order'd, and without a dole;
In all disputes, on either part he lied,
And freely pledged his oath on either side;
In all rebellions Richard join'd the rest,
In all detections Richard first confess'd:
Yet, though disgraced, he watch'd his time so well,
He rose in favour, when in fame he fell;   470
Base was his usage, vile his whole employ,
And all despised and fed the pliant boy.
At length, "'tis time he should abroad be sent,'

Was whisper'd near him,—and abroad he went;
One morn they call'd him, Richard answer'd not;
They deem'd him hanging, and in time forgot,—
Yet miss'd him long, as each, throughout the clan,
Found he 'had better spared a better man.'

Now Richard's talents for the world were fit,
He'd no small cunning, and had some small wit;   480
Had that calm look which seem'd to all assent,
And that complacent speech which nothing meant:
He'd but one care, and that he strove to hide,
How best for Richard Monday to provide.
Steel, through opposing plates, the magnet draws,
And steely atoms culls from dust and straws;
And thus our hero, to his interest true,
Gold through all bars and from each trifle drew;
But still more surely round the world to go,
This fortune's child had neither friend nor foe.   490

Long lost to us, at last our man we trace,—
Sir Richard Monday died at Monday-place:
His lady's worth, his daughter's we peruse,
And find his grandsons all as rich as Jews:
He gave reforming charities a sum,
And bought the blessings of the blind and dumb;
Bequeathed to missions money from the stocks,
And Bibles issued from his private box;
But to his native place severely just,
He left a pittance bound in rigid trust;—   500
Two paltry pounds, on every quarter's-day,
(At church produced) for forty loaves should pay;
A stinted gift, that to the parish shows
He kept in mind their bounty and their blows!

To farmers three, the year has given a son,
Finch on the Moor, and French, and Middleton.
Twice in this year a female Giles I see,
A Spalding once, and once a Barnaby:—
A humble man is he, and, when they meet,
Our farmers find him on a distant seat;   510
There for their wit he serves a constant theme,—

'They praise his dairy, they extol his team,
They ask the price of each unrivall'd steed,
And whence his sheep, that admirable breed?
His thriving arts they beg he would explain,
And where he puts the money he must gain.
They have their daughters, but they fear their friend
Would think his sons too much would condescend;—
They have their sons who would their fortunes try,
But fear his daughters will their suit deny.'   520
So runs the joke, while James, with sigh profound,
And face of care, looks moveless on the ground;
His cares, his sighs, provoke the insult more,
And point the jest—for Barnaby is poor.

   Last in my list, five untaught lads appear;
Their father dead, compassion sent them here,—
For still that rustic infidel denied
To have their names with solemn rite applied:
His, a lone house, by Deadman's Dyke-way stood;
And his, a nightly haunt, in Lonely-wood: 530
Each village inn has heard the ruffian boast,
That he believed 'in neither God nor ghost;
That, when the sod upon the sinner press'd,
He, like the saint, had everlasting rest;
That never priest believed his doctrines true,
But would, for profit, own himself a Jew,   .
Or worship wood and stone, as honest heathen do;
That fools alone on future worlds rely,
And all who die for faith, deserve to die.'
   These maxims,—part th' attorney's clerk profess'd,   540
His own transcendent genius found the rest.
Our pious matrons heard, and, much amazed,
Gazed on the man, and trembled as they gazed;
And now his face explored, and now his feet,
Man's dreaded foe, in this bad man, to meet:
But him our drunkards as their champion raised,
Their bishop call'd, and as their hero praised;
Though most, when sober, and the rest, when sick,
Had little question whence his bishopric.

But he, triumphant spirit! all things dared,   550
He poach'd the wood, and on the warren snared;
'Twas his, at cards, each novice to trepan,
And call the wants of rogues the rights of man;
Wild as the winds, he let his offspring rove,
And deem'd the marriage-bond the bane of love.
What age and sickness, for a man so bold,
Had done, we know not;—none beheld him old:
By night, as business urged, he sought the wood,—
The ditch was deep,—the rain had caused a flood,—
The foot-bridge fail'd,—he plunged beneath the deep,   560
And slept, if truth were his, th' eternal sleep.
These have we named; on life's rough sea they sail,
With many a prosperous, many an adverse gale!
Where passion soon, like powerful winds, will rage,
And prudence, wearied, with their strength engage:
Then each, in aid, shall some companion ask,
For help or comfort in the tedious task;
And what that help—what joys from union flow,
What good or ill, we next prepare to show;
And row, meantime, our weary bark ashore,   570
As Spenser his—but not with Spenser's oar.

PART III. BURIALS

. . . Old Collett of the Inn, an Instance of Dr Young's slow-sudden
Death: his Character and Conduct—The Manners and Management
of the Widow Goe: her successful Attention to Business; her Decease
unexpected. . . .

WITH Andrew Collett we the year begin,
The blind, fat landlord of the Old Crown Inn,—
Big as his butt, and, for the self-same use,
To take in stores of strong fermenting juice.
On his huge chair beside the fire he sate,
In revel chief, and umpire in debate;
Each night his string of vulgar tales he told;
When ale was cheap and bachelors were bold:
His heroes all were famous in their days,
Cheats were his boast and drunkards had his praise;   10

44

'One, in three draughts, three mugs of ale took down,
As mugs were then—the champion of the Crown;
For thrice three days another lived on ale,
And knew no change but that of mild and stale;
Two thirsty soakers watch'd a vessel's side,
When he the tap, with dexterous hand, applied;
Nor from their seats departed, till they found
That butt was out and heard the mournful sound.'

He praised a poacher, precious child of fun!
Who shot the keeper with his own spring-gun;   20
Nor less the smuggler who the exciseman tied,
And left him hanging at the birch-wood side,
There to expire;—but one who saw him hang
Cut the good cord—a traitor of the gang.

His own exploits with boastful glee he told,
What ponds he emptied and what pikes he sold;
And how, when bless'd with sight alert and gay,
The night's amusements kept him through the day.

He sang the praises of those times, when all
'For cards and dice, as for their drink, might call;   30
When justice wink'd on every jovial crew,
And ten-pins tumbled in the parson's view.'

He told, when angry wives, provoked to rail,
Or drive a third-day drunkard from his ale,
What were his triumphs, and how great the skill
That won the vex'd virago to his will;
Who raving came;—then talk'd in milder strain,—
Then wept, then drank, and pledged her spouse again.

Such were his themes: how knaves o'er laws prevail,
Or, when made captives, how they fly from jail;   40
The young how brave, how subtle were the old:
And oaths attested all that Folly told.

On death like his what name shall we bestow,
So very sudden! yet so very slow?
'Twas slow:—Disease, augmenting year by year,
Show'd the grim king by gradual steps brought near:
'Twas not less sudden; in the night he died,
He drank, he swore, he jested, and he lied;

45

Thus aiding folly with departing breath:—
'Beware, Lorenzo, the slow-sudden death.'   50
  Next died the Widow Goe, an active dame,
Famed ten miles round, and worthy all her fame;
She lost her husband when their loves were young,
But kept her farm, her credit, and her tongue:
Full thirty years she ruled, with matchless skill,
With guiding judgment and resistless will;
Advice she scorn'd, rebellions she suppress'd,
And sons and servants bow'd at her behest.
Like that great man's, who to his Saviour came,
Were the strong words of this commanding dame;—   60
'Come,' if she said, they came: if 'go,' were gone;
And if 'do this,'—that instant it was done:
Her maidens told she was all eye and ear,
In darkness saw and could at distance hear;—
No parish-business in the place could stir,
Without direction or assent from her;
In turn she took each office as it fell,
Knew all their duties, and discharged them well;
The lazy vagrants in her presence shook,
And pregnant damsels fear'd her stern rebuke;   70
She look'd on want with judgment clear and cool,
And felt with reason and bestow'd by rule;
She match'd both sons and daughters to her mind,
And lent them eyes, for Love, she heard, was blind;
Yet ceaseless still she throve, alert, alive,
The working bee, in full or empty hive;
Busy and careful, like that working bee,
No time for love nor tender cares had she;
But when our farmers made their amorous vows,
She talk'd of market-steeds and patent-ploughs.   80
Not unemploy'd her evenings pass'd away,
Amusement closed, as business waked the day;
When to her toilet's brief concern she ran,
And conversation with her friends began,
Who all were welcome, what they saw, to share;
And joyous neighbours praised her Christmas fare,

That none around might, in their scorn, complain
Of Gossip Goe as greedy in her gain.
    Thus long she reign'd, admired, if not approved;
Praised, if not honour'd; fear'd, if not beloved;—   90
When, as the busy days of Spring drew near,
That call'd for all the forecast of the year;
When lively hope the rising crops survey'd,
And April promised what September paid;
When stray'd her lambs where gorse and greenweed grow;
When rose her grass in richer vales below;
When pleas'd she look'd on all the smiling land,
And viewed the hinds, who wrought at her command;
(Poultry in groups still follow'd where she went;)
Then dread o'ercame her,—that her days were spent. 100
    'Bless me! I die, and not a warning giv'n,—
With *much* to do on Earth, and ALL for Heav'n!—
No reparation for my soul's affairs,
No leave petition'd for the barn's repairs ;
Accounts perplex'd, my interest yet unpaid,
My mind unsettled, and my will unmade;—
A lawyer haste, and in your way, a priest;
And let me die in one good work at least.'
She spake, and, trembling, dropp'd upon her knees,
Heaven in her eye and in her hand her keys;   110
And still the more she found her life decay,
With greater force she grasp'd those signs of sway:
Then fell and died!—In haste her sons drew near,
And dropp'd, in haste, the tributary tear,
Then from th' adhering clasp the keys unbound,
And consolation for their sorrows found.

From *The Borough* (1810)

Letter V

THE ELECTION

YES, our Election's past, and we've been free,
Somewhat as madmen without keepers be;

And such desire of freedom has been shown,
That both the parties wish'd her all their own:
All our free smiths and cobblers in the town
Were loth to lay such pleasant freedom down;
To put the bludgeon and cockade aside,
And let us pass unhurt and undefied.
True! you might then your party's sign produce,
And so escape with only half th' abuse;   10
With half the danger as you walk'd along,
With rage and threat'ning but from half the throng:
This you might do, and not your fortune mend,
For where you lost a foe, you gain'd a friend;
And to distress you, vex you, and expose,
Election-friends are worse than any foes;
The party-curse is with the canvass past,
But party-friendship, for your grief, will last.
Friends of all kinds, the civil and the rude,
Who humbly wish, or boldly dare t' intrude;   20
These beg or take a liberty to come,
(Friends should be free,) and make your house their home;
They know that warmly you their cause espouse,
And come to make their boastings and their bows:
You scorn their manner, you their words mistrust,
But you must hear them, and they know you must.
One plainly sees a friendship firm and true,
Between the noble candidate and you;
So humbly begs (and states at large the case),
'You'll think of Bobby and the little place.'   30
Stifling his shame by drink, a wretch will come,
And prate your wife and daughter from the room:
In pain you hear him, and at heart despise,
Yet with heroic mind your pangs disguise;
And still in patience to the sot attend,
To show what man can bear to serve a friend.
One enters hungry—not to be denied,
And takes his place and jokes—'We're of a side.'
Yet worse, the proser who, upon the strength
Of his one vote, has tales of three hours' length;   40

48

This sorry rogue you bear, yet with surprise
Start at his oaths, and sicken at his lies.
　　Then comes there one, and tells in friendly way,
What the opponents in their anger say;
All that through life has vex'd you, all abuse,
Will this kind friend in pure regard produce;
And having through your own offences run,
Adds (as appendage) what your friends have done.
　　Has any female cousin made a trip
To Gretna-Green, or more vexatious slip? 　　　　**50**
Has your wife's brother, or your uncle's son
Done aught amiss, or is he thought t' have done?
Is there of all your kindred some who lack
Vision direct, or have a gibbous back?
From your unlucky name may quips and puns
Be made by these upbraiding Goths and Huns?
To some great public character have you
Assign'd the fame to worth and talents due,
Proud of your praise?—In this, in any case,
Where the brute-spirit may affix disgrace, 　　　　60
These friends will smiling bring it, and the while
You silent sit, and practise for a smile.
　　Vain of their power, and of their value sure,
They nearly guess the tortures you endure;
Nor spare one pang—for they perceive your heart
Goes with the cause; you'd die before you'd start;
Do what they may, they're sure you'll not offend
Men who have pledged their honours to your friend.
　　Those friends indeed, who start as in a race,
May love the sport, and laugh at this disgrace; 　　　70
They have in view the glory and the prize,
Nor heed the dirty steps by which they rise:
But we their poor associates lose the fame,
Though more than partners in the toil and shame.
　　Were this the whole; and did the time produce
But shame and toil, but riot and abuse;
We might be then from serious griefs exempt,
And view the whole with pity and contempt.

Alas! but here the vilest passions rule;
It is Seduction's, is Temptation's school;   80
Where vices mingle in the oddest ways,
The grossest slander and the dirtiest praise;
Flattery enough to make the vainest sick,
And clumsy stratagem, and scoundrel trick:
Nay more, your anger and contempt to cause,
These, while they fish for profit, claim applause;
Bribed, bought and bound, they banish shame and fear;
Tell you they're staunch, and have a soul sincere;
Then talk of honour, and if doubt's express'd,
Show where it lies, and smite upon the breast.   90

Among these worthies, some at first declare
For whom they vote: he then has most to spare;
Others hang off—when coming to the post
Is spurring time, and then he'll spare the most:
While some demurring, wait, and find at last
The bidding languish, and the market pass'd;
These will affect all bribery to condemn,
And be it Satan laughs, he laughs at them.

Some too are pious—One desired the Lord
To teach him where 'to drop his little word;   100
To lend his vote, where it will profit best;
Promotion came not from the east or west;
But as their freedom had promoted some,
He should be glad to know which way 'twould come.
It was a naughty world, and where to sell
His precious charge, was more than he could tell.'

'But you succeeded?'—true, at mighty cost,
And our good friend, I fear, will think he's lost:
Inns, horses, chaises, dinners, balls and notes;
What fill'd their purses, and what drench'd their   110
    throats;
The private pension, and indulgent lease,—
Have all been granted to these friends who fleece;
Friends who will hang like burs upon his coat,
And boundless judge the value of a vote.

And though the terrors of the time be pass'd,

There still **remain** the scatterings of the blast;
The boughs are parted that entwined before,
And ancient harmony exists no more;
The gusts of wrath our peaceful seats deform,
And sadly flows the sighing of the storm: 120
Those who have gain'd are sorry for the gloom,
But they who lost, unwilling peace should come;
There open envy, here suppress'd delight,
Yet live till time shall better thoughts excite,
And so prepare us by a six-years' truce,
Again for riot, insult, and abuse.
  Our worthy mayor, on the victorious part,
Cries out for peace, and cries with all his heart;
He, civil creature! ever does his best,
To banish wrath from every voter's breast; 130
'For where,' says he, with reason strong and plain,
'Where is the profit? what will anger gain?'
His short stout person he is wont to brace
In good brown broad-cloth, edged with two-inch lace,
When in his seat; and still the coat seems new,
Preserved by common use of seaman's blue.
  He was a fisher from his earliest day,
And placed his nets within the Borough's bay;
Where by his skates, his herrings, and his soles,
He lived, nor dream'd of corporation-doles; 140
But toiling saved, and saving, never ceased
Till he had box'd up twelve score pounds at least:
He knew not money's power, but judged it best
Safe in his trunk to let his treasure rest;
Yet to a friend complain'd: 'Sad charge, to keep
So many pounds, and then I cannot sleep:'
'Then put it out,' replied the friend:—'What, give
My money up? why then I could not live:'
'Nay, but for interest place it in his hands,
Who'll give you mortgage on his house or lands.' 150
'Oh but,' said Daniel, 'that's a dangerous plan,
He may be robb'd like any other man:'
Still he is bound, and you may be at rest,

More safe the money than within your chest;
And you'll receive, from all deductions clear,
Five pounds for every hundred, every year.'
'What good in that?' quoth Daniel, 'for 'tis plain,
If part I take, there can but part remain:'
'What! you, my friend, so skill'd in gainful things,
Have you to learn what interest money brings?'   160
'Not so,' said Daniel, 'perfectly I know,
He's the most interest who has most to show.'
'True! and he'll show the more, the more he lends;
Thus he his weight and consequence extends;
For they who borrow must restore each sum,
And pay for use—What, Daniel, art thou dumb?'
For much amazed was that good man—'Indeed!
Said he with glad'ning eye, 'will money breed?
How have I lived? I grieve, with all my heart,
For my late knowledge in this precious art:—   170
Five pounds for every hundred will he give?
And then the hundred?——I begin to live.'—
So he began, and other means he found,
As he went on, to multiply a pound:
Though blind so long to interest, all allow
That no man better understands it now:
Him in our body-corporate we chose,
And once among us, he above us rose;
Stepping from post to post, he reach'd the chair,
And there he now reposes—that's the mayor.   180

   But 'tis not he, 'tis not the kinder few,
The mild, the good, who can our peace renew;
A peevish humour swells in every eye,
The warm are angry, and the cool are shy;
There is no more the social board at whist,
The good old partners are with scorn dismiss'd;
No more with dog and lantern comes the maid,
To guide the mistress when the rubber's play'd;
Sad shifts are made lest ribbons blue and green
Should at one table, at one time be seen: 190
On care and merit none will now rely,

'Tis party sells, what party-friends must buy;
The warmest burgess wears a bodger's coat,
And fashion gains less int'rest than a vote;
Uncheck'd the vintner still his poison vends,
For he too votes, and can command his friends.
    But this admitted; be it still agreed,
These ill effects from noble cause proceed;
Though like some vile excrescences they be,
The tree they spring from is a sacred tree,   **200**
And its true produce, strength and liberty.
    Yet if we could th' attendant ills suppress,
If we could make the sum of mischief less;
If we could warm and angry men persuade
No more man's common comforts to invade;
And that old ease and harmony re-seat
In all our meetings, so in joy to meet;
Much would of glory to the Muse ensue,
And our good vicar would have less to do.

Letter XIX

Position ½ way between

THE PARISH-CLERK

curate & menial church servant.

WITH our late vicar, and his age the same,
His clerk, hight Jachin, to his office came;
The like slow speech was his, the like tall slender frame:
But Jachin was the gravest man on ground,
And heard his master's jokes with look profound;
For worldly wealth this man of letters sigh'd,
And had a sprinkling of the spirit's pride:
But he was sober, chaste, devout, and just,
One whom his neighbours could believe and trust:
Of none suspected, neither man nor maid   **10**
By him were wrong'd, or were of him afraid.
    There was indeed a frown, a trick of state
In Jachin;—formal was his air and gait;
But if he seem'd more solemn and less kind,
Than some light men to light affairs confined,

Still 'twas allow'd that he should so behave
As in high seat, and be severely grave.
This book-taught man, to man's first foe profess'd
Defiance stern, and hate that knew not rest;
He held that Satan, since the world began,   20
In every act, had strife with every man;
That never evil deed on earth was done,
But of the acting parties he was one;
The flattering guide to make ill prospects clear;
To smooth rough ways the constant pioneer;
The ever-tempting, soothing, softening power,
Ready to cheat, seduce, deceive, devour.
'Me has the sly seducer oft withstood,'
Said pious Jachin,—'but he gets no good;
I pass the house where swings the tempting sign,   30
And pointing, tell him: "Satan, that is thine:"
I pass the damsels pacing down the street,
And look more grave and solemn when we meet;
Nor doth it irk me to rebuke their smiles,
Their wanton ambling and their watchful wiles:
Nay, like the good John Bunyan, when I view
Those forms, I'm angry at the ills they do;
That I could pinch and spoil, in sin's despite,
Beauties! which frail and evil thoughts excite.[1]
'At feasts and banquets seldom am I found,   40
And (save at church) abhor a tuneful sound;
To plays and shows I run not to and fro,
And where my master goes, forbear to go.'
No wonder Satan took the thing amiss,
To be opposed by such a man as this—
A man so grave, important, cautious, wise,
Who dared not trust his feeling or his eyes;
No wonder he should lurk and lie in wait,
Should fit his hooks and ponder on his bait,
Should on his movements keep a watchful eye;   50

[1] John Bunyan, in one of the many productions of his zeal, has ventured to make public this extraordinary sentiment, which the frigid piety of our clerk so readily adopted.

For he pursued a fish who led the fry.
  With his own peace our clerk was not content,
He tried, good man! to make his friends repent.
  'Nay, nay, my friends, from inns and taverns fly;
You may suppress your thirst, but not supply:
A foolish proverb says, "the devil's at home;"
But he is there, and tempts in every room:
Men feel, they know not why, such places please;
His are the spells—they're idleness and ease;
Magic of fatal kind he throws around,   60
Where care is banish'd but the heart is bound.
  'Think not of beauty; when a maid you meet,
Turn from her view and step across the street;
Dread all the sex: their looks create a charm,
A smile should fright you and a word alarm:
E'en I myself, with all my watchful care,
Have for an instant felt th' insidious snare,
And caught my sinful eyes at th' endangering stare;
Till I was forced to smite my bounding breast
With forceful blow and bid the bold-one rest.   70
  'Go not with crowds when they to pleasure run,
But public joy in private safety shun:
When bells, diverted from their true intent,
Ring loud for some deluded mortal sent
To hear or make long speech in parliament;
What time the many, that unruly beast,
Roars its rough joy and shares the final feast:
Then heed my counsel, shut thine ears and eyes;
A few will hear me—for the few are wise.'
  Not Satan's friends, nor Satan's self could bear   80
The cautious man who took of souls such care;
An interloper,—one who, out of place,
Had volunteer'd upon the side of grace:
There was his master ready once a week
To give advice; what further need he seek?
'Amen, so be it:'—what had he to do
With more than this?—'twas insolent and new;
And some determined on a way to see

How frail he was, that so it might not be.

First they essay'd to tempt our saint to sin,   90
By points of doctrine argued at an inn;
Where he might warmly reason, deeply drink,
Then lose all power to argue and to think.

In vain they tried; he took the question up,
Clear'd every doubt and barely touch'd the cup:
By many a text he proved his doctrine sound,
And look'd in triumph on the tempters round.

Next 'twas their care an artful lass to find,
Who might consult him, as perplex'd in mind;
She they conceived might put her case with fears,   100
With tender tremblings and seducing tears;
She might such charms of various kind display,
That he would feel their force and melt away:
For why of nymphs such caution and such dread,
Unless he felt and fear'd to be misled?

She came, she spake: he calmly heard her case,
And plainly told her 'twas a want of grace;
Bade her 'such fancies and affections check,
And wear a thicker muslin on her neck.'
Abased, his human foes the combat fled,   110
And the stern clerk yet higher held his head.
They were indeed a weak, impatient set,
But their shrewd prompter had his engines yet;
Had various means to make a mortal trip,
Who shunn'd a flowing bowl and rosy lip;
And knew a thousand ways his heart to move,
Who flies from banquets and who laughs at love.

Thus far the playful Muse has lent her aid,
But now departs, of graver theme afraid;
Her may we seek in more appropriate time,—   120
There is no jesting with distress and crime.

Our worthy clerk has now arrived at fame,
Such as but few in his degree might claim;
But he was poor, and wanted not the sense
That lowly rates the praise without the pence:
He saw the common herd with reverence treat

The weakest burgess whom they chanced to meet;
While few respected his exalted views,
And all beheld his doublet and his shoes:
None, when they meet, would to his parts allow   130
(Save his poor boys) a hearing or a bow:
To this false judgment of the vulgar mind,
He was not fully, as a saint, resign'd;
He found it much his jealous soul affect,
To fear derision and to find neglect.
   The year was bad, the christening-fees were small,
The weddings few, the parties paupers all:
Desire of gain with fear of want combined,
Raised sad commotion in his wounded mind;
Wealth was in all his thoughts, his views, his dreams,   140
And prompted base desires and baseless schemes.
   Alas! how often erring mortals keep
The strongest watch against the foes who sleep;
While the more wakeful, bold and artful foe
Is suffer'd guardless and unmark'd to go.
   Once in a month the sacramental bread
Our clerk with wine upon the table spread;
The custom this, that, as the vicar reads,
He for our off'rings round the church proceeds:
Tall spacious seats the wealthier people hid,   150
And none had view of what his neighbour did;
Laid on the box and mingled when they fell,
Who should the worth of each oblation tell?
Now as poor Jachin took the usual round,
And saw the alms and heard the metal sound,
He had a thought;—at first it was no more
Than—'these have cash and give it to the poor:'
A second thought from this to work began—
'And can they give it to a poorer man?'
Proceeding thus,—'My merit could they know,   160
And knew my need, how freely they'd bestow;
But though they know not, these remain the same;
And are a strong, although a secret claim:
To me, alas! the want and worth are known,

Why then, in fact, 'tis but to take my own.'
    Thought after thought pour'd in, a tempting train,—
'Suppose it done,—who is it could complain?
How could the poor? for they such trifles share,
As add no comfort, as suppress no care;
But many a pittance makes a worthy heap,—   170
What says the law? that silence puts to sleep:—
Nought then forbids, the danger could we shun,
And sure the business may be safely done.
    But am I earnest?—earnest? No.—I say,
If such my mind, that I could plan a way;
Let me reflect;—I've not allow'd me time
To purse the pieces, and if dropp'd they'd chime:'
Fertile is evil in the soul of man,—
He paused,—said Jachin, 'They may drop on bran.
Why then 'tis safe and (all consider'd) just,   180
The poor receive it,—'tis no breach of trust:
The old and widows may their trifles miss,
There must be evil in a good like this:
But I'll be kind—the sick I'll visit twice,
When now but once, and freely give advice.
Yet let me think again;'—Again he tried,
For stronger reasons on his passion's side,
And quickly these were found, yet slowly he complied.
    The morning came: the common service done,—
Shut every door,—the solemn rite begun,—   190
And, as the priest the sacred saying read,
The clerk went forward, trembling as he tread;
O'er the tall pew he held the box, and heard
The offer'd piece, rejoicing as he fear'd:
Just by the pillar, as he cautious tripp'd,
And turn'd the aisle, he then a portion slipp'd
From the full store, and to the pocket sent,
But held a moment—and then down it went.
    The priest read on, on walk'd the man afraid,
Till a gold offering in the plate was laid;   200
Trembling he took it, for a moment stopp'd,
Then down it fell, and sounded as it dropp'd;

Amazed he started, for th' affrighted man,
Lost and bewilder'd, thought not of the bran;
But all were silent, all on things intent
Of high concern, none ear to money lent;
So on he walk'd, more cautious than before,
And gain'd the purposed sum and one piece more.
  Practice makes perfect;—when the month came round,
He dropp'd the cash, nor listen'd for a sound;   210
But yet, when last of all th' assembled flock,
He ate and drank,—it gave th' electric shock:
Oft was he forced his reasons to repeat,
Ere he could kneel in quiet at his seat;
But custom soothed him—ere a single year
All this was done without restraint or fear:
Cool and collected, easy and composed,
He was correct till all the service closed;
Then to his home, without a groan or sigh,
Gravely he went, and laid his treasure by.   220
  Want will complain: some widows had express'd
A doubt if they were favour'd like the rest;
The rest described with like regret their dole,
And thus from parts they reason'd to the whole;
When all agreed some evil must be done,
Or rich men's hearts grew harder than a stone.
  Our easy vicar cut the matter short;
He would not listen to such a vile report.
  All were not thus—there govern'd in that year
A stern stout churl, an angry overseer;   230
A tyrant fond of power, loud, lewd, and most severe:
Him the mild vicar, him the graver clerk,
Advised, reproved, but nothing would he mark,
Save the disgrace, 'and that, my friends,' said he,
'Will I avenge, whenever time may be.'
And now, alas! 'twas time;—from man to man
Doubt and alarm and shrewd suspicions ran.
  With angry spirit and with sly intent,
This parish-ruler to the altar went;
A private mark he fix'd on shillings three,   240

And but one mark could in the money see;
Besides, in peering round, he chanced to note
A sprinkling slight on Jachin's Sunday-coat:
All doubt was over:—when the flock were bless'd,
In wrath he rose, and thus his mind express'd.

'Foul deeds are here!' and saying this, he took
The clerk, whose conscience, in her cold-fit, shook:
His pocket then was emptied on the place;
All saw his guilt; all witness'd his disgrace:
He fell, he fainted, not a groan, a look,   250
Escaped the culprit; 'twas a final stroke—
A death-wound never to be heal'd—a fall
That all had witness'd, and amazed were all.

As he recover'd, to his mind it came,
'I owe to Satan this disgrace and shame:'
All the seduction now appear'd in view;
'Let me withdraw,' he said, and he withdrew;
No one withheld him, all in union cried,
E'en the avenger,—'We are satisfied:'
For what has death in any form to give,   260
Equal to that man's terrors, if he live?

He lived in freedom, but he hourly saw
How much more fatal justice is than law;
He saw another in his office reign,
And his mild master treat him with disdain;
He saw that all men shunn'd him, some reviled,
The harsh pass'd frowning, and the simple smiled;
The town maintain'd him, but with some reproof,
'And clerks and scholars proudly kept aloof.'

In each lone place, dejected and dismay'd,   270
Shrinking from view, his wasting form he laid;
Or to the restless sea and roaring wind
Gave the strong yearnings of a ruin'd mind:
On the broad beach, the silent summer-day,
Stretch'd on some wreck, he wore his life away;
Or where the river mingles with the sea,
Or on the mud-bank by the elder tree,
Or by the bounding marsh-dyke, there was he:

And when unable to forsake the town,
In the blind courts he sate desponding down—   280
Always alone; then feebly would he crawl
The church-way walk, and lean upon the wall:
Too ill for this, he lay beside the door,
Compell'd to hear the reasoning of the poor:
He look'd so pale, so weak, the pitying crowd
Their firm belief of his repentance vow'd;
They saw him then so ghastly and so thin,
That they exclaim'd, 'Is this the work of sin?'
'Yes,' in his better moments, he replied,
'Of sinful avarice and the spirit's pride;—   290
While yet untempted, I was safe and well;
Temptation came; I reason'd, and I fell:
To be man's guide and glory I design'd,
A rare example for our sinful kind;
But now my weakness and my guilt I see,
And am a warning—man, be warn'd by me!'
    He said, and saw no more the human face;
To a lone loft he went, his dying place,
And, as the vicar of his state inquired,
Turn'd to the wall and silently expired!   300

Letter XXII

PETER GRIMES

OLD Peter Grimes made fishing his employ,
His wife he cabin'd with him and his boy,
And seem'd that life laborious to enjoy:
To town came quiet Peter with his fish,
And had of all a civil word and wish.
He left his trade upon the sabbath-day,
And took young Peter in his hand to pray:
But soon the stubborn boy from care broke loose,
At first refused, then added his abuse:
His father's love he scorn'd, his power defied,   10
But being drunk, wept sorely when he died.

Yes! then he wept, and to his mind there came
Much of his conduct, and he felt the shame,—
How he had oft the good old man reviled,
And never paid the duty of a child;
How, when the father in his Bible read,
He in contempt and anger left the shed:
'It is the word of life,' the parent cried;
—'This is the life itself,' the boy replied;
And while old Peter in amazement stood,   20
Gave the hot spirit to his boiling blood:—
How he, with oath and furious speech, began
To prove his freedom and assert the man;
And when the parent check'd his impious rage,
How he had cursed the tyranny of age,—
Nay, once had dealt the sacrilegious blow
On his bare head, and laid his parent low;
The father groan'd—'If thou art old,' said he,
'And hast a son—thou wilt remember me:
Thy mother left me in a happy time,   30
Thou kill'dst not her—Heav'n spares the double crime.'

On an inn-settle, in his maudlin grief,
This he revolved, and drank for his relief.

Now lived the youth in freedom, but debarr'd
From constant pleasure, and he thought it hard;
Hard that he could not every wish obey,
But must awhile relinquish ale and play;
Hard! that he could not to his cards attend,
But must acquire the money he would spend.

With greedy eye he look'd on all he saw,   40
He knew not justice, and he laugh'd at law;
On all he mark'd, he stretch'd his ready hand;
He fish'd by water and he filch'd by land:
Oft in the night has Peter dropp'd his oar,
Fled from his boat and sought for prey on shore;
Oft up the hedge-row glided, on his back
Bearing the orchard's produce in a sack,
Or farm-yard load, tugg'd fiercely from the stack;
And as these wrongs to greater numbers rose,

The more he look'd on all men as his foes.   50
   He built a mud-wall'd hovel, where he kept
His various wealth, and there he oft-times slept;
But no success could please his cruel soul,
He wish'd for one to trouble and control;
He wanted some obedient boy to stand
And bear the blow of his outrageous hand;
And hoped to find in some propitious hour
A feeling creature subject to his power.
   Peter had heard there were in London then,—
Still have they being!—workhouse-clearing men,   60
Who, undisturb'd by feelings just or kind,.
Would parish-boys to needy tradesmen bind:
They in their want a trifling sum would take,
And toiling slaves of piteous orphans make.
   Such Peter sought, and when a lad was found,
The sum was dealt him, and the slave was bound.
Some few in town observed in Peter's trap
A boy, with jacket blue and woollen cap;
But none inquired how Peter used the rope,
Or what the bruise, that made the stripling stoop;   70
None could the ridges on his back behold,
None sought him shiv'ring in the winter's cold;
None put the question,—'Peter, dost thou give
The boy his food?—What, man! the lad must live:
Consider, Peter, let the child have bread,
He'll serve thee better if he's stroked and fed.'
None reason'd thus—and some, on hearing cries,
Said calmly, 'Grimes is at his exercise.'
   Pinn'd, beaten, cold, pinch'd, threatened, and abused—
His efforts punish'd and his food refused,—   80
Awake tormented,—soon aroused from sleep,—
Struck if he wept, and yet compell'd to weep,
The trembling boy dropp'd down and strove to pray,
Received a blow, and trembling turn'd away,
Or sobb'd and hid his piteous face;—while he,
The savage master, grinn'd in horrid glee:
He'd now the power he ever loved to show,

A feeling being subject to his blow.
   Thus lived the lad, in hunger, peril, pain,
His tears despised, his supplications vain: 90
Compell'd by fear to lie, by need to steal,
His bed uneasy and unbless'd his meal,
For three sad years the boy his tortures bore,
And then his pains and trials were no more.
   'How died he, Peter?' when the people said,
He growl'd—'I found him lifeless in his bed;'
Then tried for softer tone, and sigh'd, 'Poor Sam is dead.'
Yet murmurs were there, and some questions ask'd,—
How he was fed, how punish'd, and how task'd?
Much they suspected, but they little proved,   100
And Peter pass'd untroubled and unmoved.
   Another boy with equal ease was found,
The money granted, and the victim bound;
And what his fate?—One night it chanced he fell
From the boat's mast and perish'd in her well,
Where fish were living kept, and where the boy
(So reason'd men) could not himself destroy:—
   'Yes! so it was,' said Peter, 'in his play,
(For he was idle both by night and day,)
He climb'd the main-mast and then fell below;'—   110
Then show'd his corpse and pointed to the blow:
'What said the jury?'—they were long in doubt,
But sturdy Peter faced the matter out:
So they dismiss'd him, saying at the time,
'Keep fast your hatchway when you've boys who climb.'
This hit the conscience, and he colour'd more
Than for the closest questions put before.
   Thus all his fears the verdict set aside,
And at the slave-shop Peter still applied.
   Then came a boy, of manners soft and mild,—   120
Our seamen's wives with grief beheld the child;
All thought (the poor themselves) that he was one
Of gentle blood, some noble sinner's son,
Who had, belike, deceived some humble maid,
Whom he had first seduced and then betray'd:—

64

However this, he seem'd a gracious lad,
In grief submissive and with patience sad.
    Passive he labour'd, till his slender frame
Bent with his loads, and he at length was lame:
Strange that a frame so weak could bear so long   130
The grossest insult and the foulest wrong;
But there were causes—in the town they gave
Fire, food, and comfort, to the gentle slave;
And though stern Peter, with a cruel hand,
And knotted rope, enforced the rude command,
Yet he consider'd what he'd lately felt,
And his vile blows with selfish pity dealt.
    One day such draughts the cruel fisher made,
He could not vend them in his borough-trade,
But sail'd for London-mart: the boy was ill,   140
But ever humbled to his master's will;
And on the river, where they smoothly sail'd,
He strove with terror and awhile prevail'd;
But new to danger on the angry sea,
He clung affrighten'd to his master's knee:
The boat grew leaky and the wind was strong,
Rough was the passage and the time was long;
His liquor fail'd, and Peter's wrath arose,—
No more is known—the rest we must suppose,
Or learn of Peter;—Peter says, he 'spied   150
·The stripling's danger and for harbour tried;
Meantime the fish, and then th' apprentice died.'
    The pitying women raised a clamour round,
And weeping said, 'Thou hast thy 'prentice drown'd.'
    Now the stern man was summon'd to the hall,
To tell his tale before the burghers all:
He gave th' account; profess'd the lad he loved,
And kept his brazen features all unmoved.
    The mayor himself with tone severe replied,—
'Henceforth with thee shall never boy abide;   160
Hire thee a freeman, whom thou durst not beat,
But who, in thy despite, will sleep and eat:
Free thou art now!—again shouldst thou appear,

E

Thou'lt find thy sentence, like thy soul, severe.'
    Alas! for Peter not a helping hand,
So was he hated, could he now command;
Alone he row'd his boat, alone he cast
His nets beside, or made his anchor fast;
To hold a rope or hear a curse was none,—
He toil'd and rail'd; he groan'd and swore alone.   170
    Thus by himself compell'd to live each day,
To wait for certain hours the tide's delay;
At the same times the same dull views to see,
The bounding marsh-bank and the blighted tree;
The water only, when the tides were high,
When low, the mud half-cover'd and half-dry;
The sun-burnt tar that blisters on the planks,
And bank-side stakes in their uneven ranks;
Heaps of entangled weeds that slowly float,
As the tide rolls by the impeded boat.   180
    When tides were neap, and, in the sultry day,
Through the tall bounding mud-banks made their way,
Which on each side rose swelling, and below
The dark warm flood ran silently and slow;
There anchoring, Peter chose from man to hide,
There hang his head, and view the lazy tide
In its hot slimy channel slowly glide;
Where the small eels that left the deeper way
For the warm shore, within the shallows play;
Where gaping muscles, left upon the mud,   190
Slope their slow passage to the fallen flood;—
Here dull and hopeless he'd lie down and trace
How sidelong crabs had scrawl'd their crooked race;
Or sadly listen to the tuneless cry
Of fishing gull or clanging golden-eye;
What time the sea-birds to the marsh would come,
And the loud bittern, from the bull-rush home,
Gave from the salt-ditch side the bellowing boom:
He nursed the feelings these dull scenes produce,
And loved to stop beside the opening sluice;   200
Where the small stream, confined in narrow bound,

Ran with a dull, unvaried, sadd'ning sound;
Where all, presented to the eye or ear,
Oppress'd the soul with misery, grief, and fear.
   Besides these objects, there were places three,
Which Peter seem'd with certain dread to see;
When he drew near them he would turn from each,
And loudly whistle till he pass'd the reach.
   A change of scene to him brought no relief;
In town, 'twas plain, men took him for a thief: 210
The sailors' wives would stop him in the street,
And say, 'Now, Peter, thou'st no boy to beat:'
Infants at play, when they perceived him, ran,
Warning each other—'That's the wicked man:'
He growl'd an oath, and in an angry tone
Cursed the whole place and wish'd to be alone.
   Alone he was, the same dull scenes in view,
And still more gloomy in his sight they grew:
Though man he hated, yet employ'd alone
At bootless labour, he would swear and groan,   220
Cursing the shoals that glided by the spot,
And gulls that caught them when his arts could not.
   Cold nervous tremblings shook his sturdy frame,
And strange disease—he couldn't say the name;
Wild were his dreams, and oft he rose in fright,
Waked by his view of horrors in the night,—
Horrors that would the sternest minds amaze,
Horrors that demons might be proud to raise:
And though he felt forsaken, grieved at heart,
To think he lived from all mankind apart;   230
Yet, if a man approach'd, in terrors he would start.
   A winter pass'd since Peter saw the town,
And summer-lodgers were again come down;
These, idly curious, with their glasses spied
The ships in bay as anchor'd for the tide,—
The river's craft,—the bustle of the quay,—
And sea-port views, which landmen love to see.
   One, up the river, had a man and boat
Seen day by day, now anchor'd, now afloat;

Fisher he seem'd, yet used no net nor hook;   240
Of sea-fowl swimming by no heed he took,
But on the gliding waves still fix'd his lazy look:
At certain stations he would view the stream,
As if he stood bewildered in a dream,
Or that some power had chain'd him for a time,
To feel a curse or meditate on crime.

This known, some curious, some in pity went,
And others question'd—'Wretch, dost thou repent?'
He heard, he trembled, and in fear resign'd
His boat: new terror fill'd his restless mind;   250
Furious he grew, and up the country ran,
And there they seized him—a distemper'd man:—
Him we received, and to a parish-bed,
Follow'd and cursed, the groaning man was led.

Here when they saw him, whom they used to shun,
A lost, lone man, so harass'd and undone;
Our gentle females, ever prompt to feel,
Perceived compassion on their anger steal;
His crimes they could not from their memories blot,
But they were grieved, and trembled at his lot.   260

A priest too came, to whom his words are told;
And all the signs they shudder'd to behold.

'Look! look!' they cried; 'his limbs with horror shake,
And as he grinds his teeth, what noise they make!
How glare his angry eyes, and yet he's not awake:
See! what cold drops upon his forehead stand,
And how he clenches that broad bony hand.'

The priest attending, found he spoke at times
As one alluding to his fears and crimes:
'It was the fall,' he mutter'd, 'I can show   270
The manner how—I never struck a blow:'—
And then aloud—'Unhand me, free my chain;
On oath, he fell—it struck him to the brain:—
Why ask my father?—that old man will swear
Against my life; besides, he wasn't there:—
What, all agreed?—Am I to die to-day?—
My Lord, in mercy, give me time to pray.'

Then, as they watch'd him, calmer he became,
And grew so weak he couldn't move his frame,
But murmuring spake,—while they could see and hear   280
The start of terror and the groan of fear;
See the large dew-beads on his forehead rise,
And the cold death-drop glaze his sunken eyes;
Nor yet he died, but with unwonted force
Seem'd with some fancied being to discourse:
He knew not us, or with accustom'd art
He hid the knowledge, yet exposed his heart;
'Twas part confession and the rest defence,
A madman's tale, with gleams of waking sense.

　　'I'll tell you all,' he said, 'the very day   290
When the old man first placed them in my way:
My father's spirit—he who always tried
To give me trouble, when he lived and died—
When he was gone, he could not be content
To see my days in painful labour spent,
But would appoint his meetings, and he made
Me watch at these, and so neglect my trade.

　　''Twas one hot noon, all silent, still, serene,
No living being had I lately seen;
I paddled up and down and dipp'd my net,   300
But (such his pleasure) I could nothing get,—
A father's pleasure, when his toil was done,
To plague and torture thus an only son!
And so I sat and look'd upon the stream,
How it ran on, and felt as in a dream:
But dream it was not; no!—I fix'd my eyes
On the mid stream and saw the spirits rise;
I saw my father on the water stand,
And hold a thin pale boy in either hand;
And there they glided ghastly on the top   310
Of the salt flood, and never touch'd a drop:
I would have struck them, but they knew th' intent,
And smiled upon the oar, and down they went.

　　'Now, from that day, whenever I began
To dip my net, there stood the hard old man—

He and those boys: I humbled me and pray'd
They would be gone;—they heeded not, but stay'd:
Nor could I turn, nor would the boat go by,
But gazing on the spirits, there was I:
They bade me leap to death, but I was loth to die: 320
And every day, as sure as day arose,
Would these three spirits meet me ere the close;
To hear and mark them daily was my doom,
And "Come," they said, with weak, sad voices, "come."
To row away with all my strength I try'd,
But there were they, hard by me in the tide,
The three unbodied forms—and "Come," still "come,"
    they cried.

   'Fathers should pity—but this old man shook
His hoary locks, and froze me by a look:
Thrice, when I struck them, through the water came   330
A hollow groan, that weaken'd all my frame:
"Father!" said I, "have mercy:"—He replied,
I know not what—the angry spirit lied,—
"Didst thou not draw thy knife?" said he:—'Twas true.
But I had pity and my arm withdrew:
He cried for mercy which I kindly gave,
But he has no compassion in his grave.

   'There were three places, where they ever rose,—
The whole long river has not such as those,—
Places accursed, where, if a man remain,   340
He'll see the things which strike him to the brain;
And there they made me on my paddle lean,
And look at them for hours;—accursed scene!
When they would glide to that smooth eddy-space,
Then bid me leap and join them in the place;
And at my groans each little villain sprite
Enjoy'd my pains and vanish'd in delight.

   'In one fierce summer-day, when my poor brain
Was burning hot and cruel was my pain,
Then came this father-foe, and there he stood   350
With his two boys again upon the flood;
There was more mischief in their eyes, more glee

In their pale faces when they glared at me:
Still did they force me on the oar to rest,
And when they saw me fainting and oppress'd,
He, with his hand, the old man, scoop'd the flood,
And there came flame about him mix'd with blood;
He bade me stoop and look upon the place,
Then flung the hot-red liquor in my face;
Burning it blazed, and then I roar'd for pain,   360
I thought the demons would have turn'd my brain.
  'Still there they stood, and forced me to behold
A place of horrors—they cannot be told—
Where the flood open'd, there I heard the shriek
Of tortured guilt—no earthly tongue can speak:
"All days alike! for ever!" did they say,
"And unremitted torments every day"—
Yes, so they said:'—But here he ceased and gazed
On all around, affrighten'd and amazed;
And still he tried to speak, and look'd in dread   370
Of frighten'd females gathering round his bed;
Then dropp'd exhausted and appear'd at rest,
Till the strong foe the vital powers possess'd;
Then with an inward, broken voice he cried,
'Again they come,' and mutter'd as he died.

From *Tales in Verse* (1812)

PROCRASTINATION

LOVE will expire, the gay, the happy dream
Will turn to scorn, indiff'rence, or esteem:
Some favour'd pairs, in this exchange, are blest,
Nor sigh for raptures in a state of rest;
Others, ill match'd, with minds unpair'd, repent
At once the deed, and know no more content;
From joy to anguish they, in haste, decline,
And with their fondness, their esteem resign:
More luckless still their fate, who are the prey
Of long-protracted hope and dull delay;   10

71

'Mid plans of bliss the heavy hours pass on,
Till love is wither'd, and till joy is gone.

This gentle flame two youthful hearts possess'd,
The sweet disturber of unenvied rest:
The prudent Dinah was the maid beloved,
And the kind Rupert was the swain approved:
A wealthy aunt her gentle niece sustain'd,
He, with a father, at his desk remain'd;
The youthful couple, to their vows sincere,
Thus loved expectant; year succeeding year,   20
With pleasant views and hopes, but not a prospect near.
Rupert some comfort in his station saw,
But the poor virgin lived in dread and awe;
Upon her anxious looks the widow smiled,
And bade her wait, 'for she was yet a child.'
She for her neighbour had a due respect,
Nor would his son encourage or reject;
And thus the pair, with expectations vain,
Beheld the seasons change and change again:
Meantime the nymph her tender tales perused,   30
Where cruel aunts impatient girls refused;
While hers, though teasing, boasted to be kind,
And she, resenting, to be all resign'd.

The dame was sick, and when the youth applied
For her consent, she groan'd, and cough'd, and cried:
Talk'd of departing, and again her breath
Drew hard, and cough'd, and talk'd again of death:
'Here you may live, my Dinah! here the boy
And you together my estate enjoy;'
Thus to the lovers was her mind express'd,   40
Till they forbore to urge the fond request.

Servant, and nurse, and comforter, and friend,
Dinah had still some duty to attend;
But yet their walk, when Rupert's evening call
Obtain'd an hour, made sweet amends for all;
So long they now each other's thoughts had known,

That nothing seem'd exclusively their own;
But with the common wish, the mutual fear,
They now had travell'd to their thirtieth year.

At length a prospect open'd—but, alas!   50
Long time must yet, before the union, pass;
Rupert was call'd in other clime, t'increase
Another's wealth, and toil for future peace;
Loth were the lovers; but the aunt declared
'Twas fortune's call, and they must be prepared;
'You now are young, and for this brief delay,
And Dinah's care, what I bequeath will pay;
All will be yours; nay, love, suppress that sigh;
The kind must suffer, and the best must die:'
Then came the cough, and strong the signs it gave   60
Of holding long contention with the grave.

The lovers parted with a gloomy view,
And little comfort but that both were true;
He for uncertain duties doom'd to steer,
While hers remain'd too certain and severe.

Letters arrived, and Rupert fairly told
'His cares were many, and his hopes were cold;
The view more clouded, that was never fair,
And love alone preserved him from despair:'
In other letters brighter hopes he drew,   70
'His friends were kind, and he believed them true.'

When the sage widow Dinah's grief descried,
She wonder'd much why one so happy sigh'd:
Then bade her see how her poor aunt sustain'd
The ills of life, nor murmur'd nor complain'd.
To vary pleasures, from the lady's chest
Were drawn the pearly string and tabby vest;
Beads, jewels, laces, all their value shown,
With the kind notice—'They will be your own.'

This hope, these comforts cherish'd by by day,   80
To Dinah's bosom made a gradual way;

73

Till love of treasure had as large a part,
As love of Rupert, in the virgin's heart.
Whether it be that tender passions fail,
From their own nature, while the strong prevail;
Or whether av'rice, like the poison-tree,[1]
Kills all beside it, and alone will be;
Whatever cause prevail'd, the pleasure grew
In Dinah's soul,—she loved the hoards to view;
With lively joy those comforts she survey'd,   90
And love grew languid in the careful maid.

Now the grave niece partook the widow's cares,
Look'd to the great and ruled the small affairs;
Saw clean'd the plate, arranged the china show,
And felt her passion for a shilling grow:
Th' indulgent aunt increased the maid's delight,
By placing tokens of her wealth in sight;
She loved the value of her bonds to tell,
And spake of stocks, and how they rose and fell.

This passion grew, and gain'd at length such sway,   100
That other passions shrank to make it way;
Romantic notions now the heart forsook,
She read but seldom, and she changed her book;
And for the verses she was wont to send,
Short was her prose, and she was Rupert's friend.
Seldom she wrote, and then the widow's cough,
And constant call, excused her breaking off;
Who, now, oppress'd no longer took the air,
But sate and dozed upon an easy chair.
The cautious doctor saw the case was clear,   110
But judged it best to have companions near;
They came, they reason'd, they prescribed—at last,
Like honest men, they said their hopes were past;
Then came a priest—'tis comfort to reflect,

---

[1] Allusion is here made, not to the well-known species of *sumach*, called the poison oak, or *toxicodendron*, but to the *upas*, or poison-tree of Java: whether it be real or imaginary, this is no proper place for inquiry.

When all is over, there was no neglect;
And all was over—by her husband's bones,
The widow rests beneath the sculptured stones,
That yet record their fondness and their fame,
While all they left the virgin's care became;
Stock, bonds, and buildings;—it disturb'd her rest,   120
To think what load of troubles she possess'd:
Yet, if a trouble, she resolved to take
Th' important duty, for the donor's sake;
She too was heiress to the widow's taste,
Her love of hoarding, and her dread of waste.

Sometimes the past would on her mind intrude,
And then a conflict full of care ensued;
The thoughts of Rupert on her mind would press,
His worth she knew, but doubted his success;
Of old she saw him heedless; what the boy   130
Forbore to save, the man would not enjoy;
Oft had he lost the chance that care would seize,
Willing to live, but more to live at ease:
Yet could she not a broken vow defend,
And Heav'n, perhaps, might yet enrich her friend.

Month after month was pass'd, and all were spent
In quiet comfort and in rich content:
Miseries there were, and woes the world around,
But these had not her pleasant dwelling found;
She knew that mothers grieved, and widows wept,   140
And she was sorry, said her prayers, and slept:
Thus pass'd the seasons, and to Dinah's board
Gave what the seasons to the rich afford;
For she indulged, nor was her heart so small,
That one strong passion should engross it all.

A love of splendour now with av'rice strove,
And oft appear'd to be the stronger love:
A secret pleasure fill'd the widow's breast,
When she reflected on the hoards possess'd;

But livelier joy inspired th' ambitious maid,   150
When she the purchase of those hoards display'd:
In small but splendid room she loved to see
That all was placed in view and harmony;
There, as with eager glance she look'd around,
She much delight in every object found;
While books devout were near her—to destroy,
Should it arise, an overflow of joy.

   Within that fair apartment, guests might see
The comforts cull'd for wealth by vanity:
Around the room an Indian paper blazed,   160
With lively tint and figures boldly raised;
Silky and soft upon the floor below,
Th' elastic carpet rose with crimson glow;
All things around implied both cost and care,
What met the eye was elegant or rare:
Some curious trifles round the room were laid,
By hope presented to the wealthy maid:
Within a costly case of varnish'd wood,
In level rows, her polish'd volumes stood;
Shown as a favour to a chosen few,   170
To prove what beauty for a book could do:
A silver urn with curious work was fraught;
A silver lamp from Grecian pattern wrought:
Above her head, all gorgeous to behold,
A time-piece stood on feet of burnish'd gold;
A stag's-head crest adorn'd the pictured case,
Through the pure crystal shone the enamell'd face;
And while on brilliants moved the hands of steel,
It click'd from pray'r to pray'r, from meal to meal.

   Here as the lady sate, a friendly pair   180
Stept in t' admire the view, and took their chair:
They then related how the young and gay
Were thoughtless wandering in the broad highway;
How tender damsels sail'd in tilted boats,
And laugh'd with wicked men in scarlet coats;

And how we live in such degen'rate times,
That men conceal their wants, and show their crimes;
While vicious deeds are screen'd by fashion's name,
And what was once our pride is now our shame.

Dinah was musing, as her friends discoursed,   190
When these last words a sudden entrance forced
Upon her mind, and what was once her pride
And now her shame, some painful views supplied;
Thoughts of the past within her bosom press'd,
And there a change was felt, and was confess'd:
While thus the virgin strove with secret pain,
Her mind was wandering o'er the troubled main;
Still she was silent, nothing seem'd to see,
But sate and sigh'd in pensive reverie.

The friends prepared new subjects to begin,   200
When tall Susannah, maiden starch, stalk'd in;
Not in her ancient mode, sedate and slow,
As when she came, the mind she knew, to know;
Nor as, when list'ning half an hour before,
She twice or thrice tapp'd gently at the door;
But, all decorum cast in wrath aside,
'I think the devil's in the man!' she cried;
'A huge tall sailor, with his tawny cheek,
And pitted face, will with my lady speak;
He grinn'd an ugly smile, and said he knew,   210
Please you, my lady, 'twould be joy to you:
What must I answer?'—Trembling and distress'd
Sank the pale Dinah by her fears oppress'd;
When thus alarm'd, and brooking no delay,
Swift to her room the stranger made his way.

'Revive, my love!' said he, 'I've done thee harm,
'Give me thy pardon,' and he look'd alarm:
Meantime the prudent Dinah had contrived
Her soul to question, and she then revived.

'See! my good friend,' and then she raised her head, 220
'The bloom of life, the strength of youth is fled;

Living we die; to us the world is dead;
We parted bless'd with health, and I am now
Age-struck and feeble, so I find art thou;
Thine eye is sunken, furrow'd is thy face,
And downward look'st thou—so we run our race;
And happier they, whose race is nearly run,
Their troubles over, and their duties done.'

'True, lady, true, we are not girl and boy;
But time has left us something to enjoy.'   230

'What! thou hast learn'd my fortune?—yes, I live
To feel how poor the comforts wealth can give;
Thou too perhaps art wealthy; but our fate
Still mocks our wishes, wealth is come too late.'

'To me nor late nor early; I am come
Poor as I left thee to my native home:
Nor yet,' said Rupert, 'will I grieve; 'tis mine
To share thy comforts, and the glory thine;
For thou wilt gladly take that generous part
That both exalts and gratifies the heart;   240
While mine rejoices'—'Heavens!' return'd the maid,
'This talk to one so wither'd and decay'd?
No! all my care is now to find my mind
For other spousal, and to die resign'd:
As friend and neighbour, I shall hope to see
These noble views, this pious love in thee;
That we together may the change await,
Guides and spectators in each other's fate;
When fellow-pilgrims, we shall daily crave
The mutual prayer that arms us for the grave.'   250

Half angry, half in doubt, the lover gazed
On the meek maiden, by her speech amazed;
'Dinah,' said he, 'dost thou respect thy vows?
What spousal mean'st thou?—thou art Rupert's spouse:
The chance is mine to take, and thine to give;

But, trifling this, if we together live:
Can I believe, that, after all the past,
Our vows, our loves, thou wilt be false at last?
Something thou hast—I know not what—in view;
I find thee pious—let me find thee true.'   260

   'Ah! cruel this; but do, my friend, depart;
And to its feelings leave my wounded heart.'

   'Nay, speak at once; and Dinah, let me know,
Mean'st thou to take me, now I'm wrecked, in tow?
Be fair; nor longer keep me in the dark;
Am I forsaken for a trimmer spark?
Heaven's spouse thou art not; nor can I believe
That God accepts her who will man deceive:
True I am shatter'd, I have service seen,
And service done, and have in trouble been;   270
My cheek (it shames me not) has lost its red,
And the brown buff is o'er my features spread;
Perchance my speech is rude; for I among
Th' untamed have been, in temper and in tongue;
Have been trepann'd, have lived in toil and care,
And wrought for wealth I was not doom'd to share;
It touch'd me deeply, for I felt a pride
In gaining riches for my destined bride:
Speak then my fate; for these my sorrows past,
Time lost, youth fled, hope wearied, and at last   280
This doubt of thee—a childish thing to tell,
But certain truth—my very throat they swell;
They stop the breath, and but for shame could I
Give way to weakness, and with passion cry;
These are unmanly struggles, but I feel
This hour must end them, and perhaps will heal."—

   Here Dinah sigh'd as if afraid to speak—
And then repeated—"They were frail and weak;
His soul she loved, and hoped he had the grace
To fix his thoughts upon a better place."   290

79

She ceased;—with steady glance, as if to see
The very root of this hypocrisy,—
He her small fingers moulded in his hard
And bronzed broad hand; then told her his regard,
His best respect were gone, but love had still
Hold in his heart, and govern'd yet the will—
Or he would curse her:—saying this, he threw
The hand in scorn away, and bade adieu
To every lingering hope, with every care in view.

Proud and indignant, suffering, sick, and poor,   300
He grieved unseen; and spoke of love no more—
Till all he felt in indignation died,
As hers had sunk in avarice and pride.

In health declining, as in mind distress'd,
To some in power his troubles he confess'd,
And shares a parish-gift;—at prayers he sees
The pious Dinah dropp'd upon her knees;
Thence as she walks the street with stately air,
As chance directs, oft meet the parted pair:
When he, with thickset coat of badge-man's blue,   310
Moves near her shaded silk of changeful hue;
When his thin locks of grey approach her braid,
A costly purchase made in beauty's aid;
When his frank air, and his unstudied pace,
Are seen with her soft manner, air, and grace,
And his plain artless look with her sharp meaning face;
It might some wonder in a stranger move,
How these together could have talk'd of love.

Behold them now!—see there a tradesman stands,
And humbly hearkens to some fresh commands;   320
He moves to speak, she interrupts him—'Stay,'
Her air expresses—'Hark! to what I say:'
Ten paces off, poor Rupert on a seat
Has taken refuge from the noon-day heat,
His eyes on her intent, as if to find
What were the movements of that subtle mind:

How still!—how earnest is he!—it appears
His thoughts are wand'ring through his earlier years;
Through years of fruitless labour, to the day
When all his earthly prospects died away: 330
'Had I,' he thinks, 'been wealthier of the two,
Would she have found me so unkind, untrue?
Or knows not man when poor, what man when rich
    will do?
Yes, yes! I feel that I had faithful proved,
And should have soothed and raised her, bless'd and
    loved.'

  But Dinah moves—she had observed before
The pensive Rupert at an humble door:
Some thoughts of pity raised by his distress,
Some feeling touch of ancient tenderness;
Religion, duty urged the maid to speak   340
In terms of kindness to a man so weak:
But pride forbad, and to return would prove
She felt the shame of his neglected love;
Nor wrapp'd in silence could she pass, afraid
Each eye should see her, and each heart upbraid;
One way remain'd—the way the Levite took,
Who without mercy could on misery look;
(A way perceived by craft, approved by pride),
She cross'd, and pass'd him on the other side.

THE FRANK COURTSHIP

GRAVE Jonas Kindred, Sybil Kindred's sire,
Was six feet high, and look'd six inches higher;
Erect, morose, determined, solemn, slow,
Who knew the man, could never cease to know;
His faithful spouse, when Jonas was not by,
Had a firm presence and a steady eye;
But with her husband dropp'd her look and tone,
And Jonas ruled unquestion'd and alone.

He read, and oft would quote the sacred words,
How pious husbands of their wives were lords;   10
Sarah call'd Abraham Lord! and who could be,
So Jonas thought, a greater man than he?
Himself he view'd with undisguised respect,
And never pardon'd freedom or neglect.

They had one daughter, and this favourite child
Had oft the father of his spleen beguiled;
Soothed by attention from her early years,
She gain'd all wishes by her smiles or tears:
But Sybil then was in that playful time,
When contradiction is not held a crime;   20
When parents yield their children idle praise
For faults corrected in their after days.

Peace in the sober house of Jonas dwelt,
Where each his duty and his station felt:
Yet not that peace some favour'd mortals find,
In equal views and harmony of mind;
Not the soft peace that blesses those who love,
Where all with one consent in union move;
But it was that which one superior will
Commands, by making all inferiors still;   30
Who bids all murmurs, all objections cease,
And with imperious voice announces—Peace!

They were, to wit, a remnant of that crew,
Who, as their foes maintain, their sovereign slew;
An independent race, precise, correct,
Who ever married in the kindred sect:
No son or daughter of their order wed
A friend to England's king who lost his head;
Cromwell was still their saint, and when they met,
They mourn'd that saints [1] were not our rulers yet.   40

[1] This appellation is here used not ironically, nor with malignity; but it is taken merely to designate a morosely devout people, with peculiar austerity of manners.

Fix'd were their habits; they arose betimes,
Then pray'd their hour, and sang their party-rhymes:
Their meals were plenteous, regular, and plain;
The trade of Jonas brought him constant gain;
Vender of hops and malt, of coals and corn—
And, like his father, he was merchant born:
Neat was their house; each table, chair, and stool,
Stood in its place, or moving moved by rule;
No lively print or picture graced the room;
A plain brown paper lent its decent gloom;   50
But here the eye, in glancing round, survey'd
A small recess that seem'd for china made;
Such pleasing pictures seem'd this pencill'd ware,
That few would search for nobler objects there—
Yet, turn'd by chosen friends, and there appear'd
His stern, strong features, whom they all revered;
For there in lofty air was seen to stand
The bold Protector of the conquer'd land;
Drawn in that look with which he wept and swore,
Turn'd out the Members, and made fast the door,   60
Ridding the House of every knave and drone,
Forced, though it grieved his soul, to rule alone.
The stern still smile each friend approving gave,
Then turn'd the view, and all again were grave.

There stood a clock, though small the owner's need,
For habit told when all things should proceed;
Few their amusements, but when friends appear'd,
They with the world's distress their spirits cheer'd;
The nation's guilt, that would not long endure
The reign of men so modest and so pure: 70
Their town was large, and seldom pass'd a day
But some had fail'd, and others gone astray;
Clerks had absconded, wives eloped, girls flown
To Gretna-Green, or sons rebellious grown;
Quarrels and fires arose;—and it was plain
The times were bad; the saints had ceased to reign!

A few yet lived to languish and to mourn
For good old manners never to return.

Jonas had sisters, and of these was one
Who lost a husband and an only son: 80
Twelve months her sables she in sorrow wore,
And mourn'd so long that she could mourn no more.
Distant from Jonas, and from all her race,
She now resided in a lively place;
There, by the sect unseen, at whist she play'd,
Nor was of churchmen or their church afraid:
If much of this the graver brother heard,
He something censured, but he little fear'd;
He knew her rich and frugal; for the rest,
He felt no care, or, if he felt, suppress'd: 90
Nor for companion when she ask'd her niece,
Had he suspicions that disturb'd his peace;
Frugal and rich, these virtues as a charm
Preserved the thoughtful man from all alarm;
An infant yet, she soon would home return,
Nor stay the manners of the world to learn;
Meantime his boys would all his care engross,
And be his comforts if he felt the loss.

The sprightly Sybil, pleased and unconfined,
Felt the pure pleasure of the op'ning mind: 100
All here was gay and cheerful—all at home
Unvaried quiet and unruffled gloom:
There were no changes, and amusements few;
Here, all was varied, wonderful, and new;
There were plain meals, plain dresses, and grave looks—
Here, gay companions and amusing books;
And the young beauty soon began to taste
The light vocations of the scene she graced.

A man of business feels it as a crime
On calls domestic to consume his time;   110
Yet this grave man had not so cold a heart,

But with his daughter he was grieved to part:
And he demanded that in every year
The aunt and niece should at his house appear.

'Yes! we must go, my child, and by our dress
A grave conformity of mind express;
Must sing at meeting, and from cards refrain,
The more t' enjoy when we return again.'

Thus spake the aunt, and the discerning child
Was pleased to learn how fathers are beguiled.   120
Her artful part the young dissembler took,
And from the matron caught th' approving look:
When thrice the friends had met, excuse was sent
For more delay, and Jonas was content;
Till a tall maiden by her sire was seen,
In all the bloom and beauty of sixteen;
He gazed admiring;—she, with visage prim,
Glanced an arch look of gravity on him;
For she was gay at heart, but wore disguise,
And stood a vestal in her father's eyes: 130
Pure, pensive, simple, sad; the damsel's heart,
When Jonas praised, reproved her for the part;
For Sybil, fond of pleasure, gay and light,
Had still a secret bias to the right;
Vain as she was—and flattery made her vain—
Her simulation gave her bosom pain.

Again return'd, the matron and the niece
Found the late quiet gave their joy increase;
The aunt infirm, no more her visits paid,
But still with her sojourn'd the favourite maid.   140
Letters were sent when franks could be procured,
And when they could not, silence was endured;
All were in health, and if they older grew,
It seem'd a fact that none among them knew;
The aunt and niece still led a pleasant life,
And quiet days had Jonas and his wife.

Near him a widow dwelt of worthy fame,
Like his her manners, and her creed the same;
The wealth her husband left, her care retain'd
For one tall youth, and widow she remain'd;   150
His love respectful all her care repaid,
Her wishes watch'd, and her commands obey'd.

Sober he was and grave from early youth,
Mindful of forms, but more intent on truth;
In a light drab he uniformly dress'd,
And look serene th' unruffled mind express'd;
A hat with ample verge his brows o'erspread,
And his brown locks curl'd graceful on his head;
Yet might observers in his speaking eye
Some observation, some acuteness spy;   160
The friendly thought it keen, the treacherous deem'd
     it sly;
Yet not a crime could foe or friend detect,
His actions all were, like his speech, correct;
And they who jested on a mind so sound,
Upon his virtues must their laughter found;
Chaste, sober, solemn, and devout they named
Him who was thus, and not of *this* ashamed.

Such were the virtues Jonas found in one
In whom he warmly wish'd to find a son:
Three years had pass'd since he had Sybil seen;   170
But she was doubtless what she once had been,
Lovely and mild, obedient and discreet;
The pair must love whenever they should meet;
Then ere the widow or her son should choose
Some happier maid, he would explain his views:
Now she, like him, was politic and shrewd,
With strong desire of lawful gain embued;
To all he said, she bow'd with much respect,
Pleased to comply, yet seeming to reject;
Cool and yet eager, each admired the strength   180
Of the opponent, and agreed at length:

86

As a drawn battle shows to each a force,
Powerful as his, he honours it of course;
So in these neighbours, each the power discern'd,
And gave the praise that was to each return'd.

Jonas now ask'd his daughter—and the aunt,
Though loth to lose her, was obliged to grant:—
But would not Sybil to the matron cling,
And fear to leave the shelter of her wing?
No! in the young there lives a love of change,   190
And to the easy they prefer the strange!
Then too the joys she once pursued with zeal,
From whist and visits sprung, she ceased to feel:
When with the matrons Sybil first sat down,
To cut for partners and to stake her crown,
This to the youthful maid preferment seem'd,
Who thought what woman she was then esteem'd;
But in few years, when she perceived, indeed,
The real woman to the girl succeed,
No longer tricks and honours fill'd her mind,   200
But other feelings, not so well defined;
She then reluctant grew, and thought it hard,
To sit and ponder o'er an ugly card;
Rather the nut-tree shade the nymph preferr'd,
Pleased with the pensive gloom and evening bird;
Thither, from company retired, she took
The silent walk, or read the fav'rite book.

The father's letter, sudden, short, and kind,
Awaked her wonder, and disturb'd her mind;
She found new dreams upon her fancy seize,   210
Wild roving thoughts and endless reveries:
The parting came;—and when the aunt perceived
The tears of Sybil, and how much she grieved—
To love for her that tender grief she laid,
That various, soft, contending passions made.

When Sybil rested in her father's arms,
His pride exulted in a daughter's charms;

A maid accomplish'd he was pleased to find,
Nor seem'd the form more lovely than the mind:
But when the fit of pride and fondness fled,   220
He saw his judgment by his hopes misled;
High were the lady's spirits, far more free
Her mode of speaking than a maid's should be;
Too much, as Jonas thought, she seem'd to know,
And all her knowledge was disposed to show;
'Too gay her dress, like theirs who idly dote
On a young coxcomb, or a coxcomb's coat;
In foolish spirits when our friends appear,
And vainly grave when not a man is near.'

Thus Jonas, adding to his sorrow blame,   230
And terms disdainful to his sister's name:—
'The sinful wretch has by her arts defiled
The ductile spirit of my darling child.'

'The maid is virtuous,' said the dame—Quoth he,
'Let her give proof, by acting virtuously:
Is it in gaping when the Elders pray?
In reading nonsense half a summer's day?
In those mock forms that she delights to trace,
Or her loud laughs in Hezekiah's face?
She—O Susannah!—to the world belongs;   240
She loves the follies of its idle throngs,
And reads soft tales of love, and sing's love's soft'ning songs.
But as our friend is yet delay'd in town,
We must prepare her till the youth comes down;
You shall advise the maiden; I will threat;
Her fears and hopes may yield us comfort yet.'

Now the grave father took the lass aside,
Demanding sternly, 'Wilt thou be a bride?'
She answer'd, calling up an air sedate,
'I have not vow'd against the holy state.'   250

'No folly, Sybil,' said the parent; 'know
What to their parents virtuous maidens owe:

A worthy, wealthy youth, whom I approve,
Must thou prepare to honour and to love.
Formal to thee his air and dress may seem,
But the good youth is worthy of esteem:
Shouldst thou with rudeness treat him; of disdain
Should he with justice or of slight complain,
Or of one taunting speech give certain proof,
Girl! I reject thee from my sober roof.'   260

'My aunt,' said Sybil, 'will with pride protect
One whom a father can for this reject;
Nor shall a formal, rigid, soul-less boy
My manners alter, or my views destroy!'

Jonas then lifted up his hands on high,
And utt'ring something 'twixt a groan and sigh,
Left the determined maid, her doubtful mother by.

'Hear me,' she said; 'incline thy heart, my child,
And fix thy fancy on a man so mild:
Thy father, Sybil, never could be moved   270
By one who loved him, or by one he loved.
Union like ours is but a bargain made
By slave and tyrant—he will be obey'd;
Then calls the quiet, comfort—but thy youth
Is mild by nature, and as frank as truth.'

'But will he love?' said Sybil; 'I am told
That these mild creatures are by nature cold.'

'Alas!' the matron answer'd, 'much I dread
That dangerous love by which the young are led!
That love is earthy; you the creature prize,   280
And trust your feelings and believe your eyes:
Can eyes and feelings inward worth descry?
No! my fair daughter, on our choice rely!
Your love, like that display'd upon the stage,
Indulged is folly, and opposed is rage;—

More prudent love our sober couples show,
All that to mortal beings, mortals owe;
All flesh is grass—before you give a heart,
Remember, Sybil, that in death you part;
And should your husband die before your love,   290
What needless anguish must a widow prove!
No! my fair child, let all such visions cease;
Yield but esteem, and only try for peace.'

'I must be loved,' said Sybil; 'I must see
The man in terrors who aspires to me;
At my forbidding frown, his heart must ache,
His tongue must falter, and his frame must shake:
And if I grant him at my feet to kneel,
What trembling, fearful pleasure must he feel;
Nay, such the raptures that my smiles inspire,   300
That reason's self must for a time retire.'

'Alas! for good Josiah,' said the dame,
'These wicked thoughts would fill his soul with shame;
He kneel and tremble at a thing of dust!
He cannot, child:'—the child replied, 'He must.'

They ceased: the matron left her with a frown;
So Jonas met her when the youth came down:
'Behold,' said he, 'thy future spouse attends;
Receive him, daughter, as the best of friends;
Observe, respect him—humble be each word,   310
That welcomes home thy husband and thy lord.'

Forewarn'd, thought Sybil, with a bitter smile,
I shall prepare my manner and my style.

Ere yet Josiah enter'd on his task,
The father met him—'Deign to wear a mask
A few dull days, Josiah—but a few—
It is our duty, and the sex's due;
I wore it once, and every grateful wife

Repays it with obedience through her life:
Have no regard to Sybil's dress, have none   320
To her pert language, to her flippant tone:
Henceforward thou shalt rule unquestion'd and alone;
And she thy pleasure in thy looks shall seek—
How she shall dress, and whether she may speak.'

   A sober smile return'd the youth, and said,
'Can I cause fear, who am myself afraid?'

   Sybil, meantime, sat thoughtful in her room,
And often wonder'd—'Will the creature come?
Nothing shall tempt, shall force me to bestow
My hand upon him—yet I wish to know.'   330

   The door unclosed, and she beheld her sire
Lead in the youth, then hasten to retire;
'Daughter, my friend—my daughter, friend'—he cried,
And gave a meaning look, and stepp'd aside;
That look contain'd a mingled threat and prayer,
'Do take him, child—offend him if you dare.'

   The couple gazed—were silent, and the maid
Look'd in his face, to make the man afraid;
The man, unmoved, upon the maiden cast
A steady view—so salutation pass'd: 340
But in this instant Sybil's eye had seen
The tall fair person, and the still staid mien;
The glow that temp'rance o'er the cheek had spread,
Where the soft down half veil'd the purest red;
And the serene deportment that proclaim'd
A heart unspotted, and a life unblamed:
But then with these she saw attire too plain,
The pale brown coat, though worn without a stain;
The formal air, and something of the pride
That indicates the wealth it seems to hide;   350
And looks that were not, she conceived, exempt
From a proud pity, or a sly contempt.

Josiah's eyes had their employment too,
Engaged and soften'd by so bright a view;
A fair and meaning face, an eye of fire,
That check'd the bold, and made the free retire:
But then with these he mark'd the studied dress
And lofty air, that scorn or pride express;
With that insidious look, that seem'd to hide
In an affected smile the scorn and pride;   360
And if his mind the virgin's meaning caught,
He saw a foe with treacherous purpose fraught—
Captive the heart to take, and to reject it caught.

Silent they sate—thought Sybil, that he seeks
Something, no doubt; I wonder if he speaks:
Scarcely she wonder'd, when these accents fell
Slow in her ear—'Fair maiden, art thou well?'
'Art thou physician?' she replied; 'my hand,
My pulse, at least, shall be at thy command.'

She said—and saw, surprised, Josiah kneel,   370
And gave his lips the offer'd pulse to feel;
The rosy colour rising in her cheek,
Seem'd that surprise unmix'd with wrath to speak;
Then sternness she assumed, and—'Doctor, tell,
Thy words cannot alarm me—am I well?'

'Thou art,' said he; 'and yet thy dress so light,
I do conceive, some danger must excite:'
'In whom?' said Sybil, with a look demure:
'In more,' said he, 'than I expect to cure.
I, in thy light luxuriant robe, behold   380
Want and excess, abounding and yet cold;
Here needed, there display'd, in many a wanton fold:
Both health and beauty, learned authors show,
From a just medium in our clothing flow.'

'Proceed, good doctor; if so great my need,
What is thy fee? Good doctor! pray proceed.'

'Large is my fee, fair lady, but I take
None till some progress in my cure I make:
Thou hast disease, fair maiden; thou art vain;
Within that face sit insult and disdain;   390
Thou art enamour'd of thyself; my art
Can see the naughty malice of thy heart:
With a strong pleasure would thy bosom move,
Were I to own thy power, and ask thy love;
And such thy beauty, damsel, that I might,
But for thy pride, feel danger in thy sight,
And lose my present peace in dreams of vain delight.'

'And can thy patients,' said the nymph, 'endure
Physic like this? and will it work a cure?'

'Such is my hope, fair damsel; thou, I find,   400
Hast the true tokens of a noble mind;
But the world wins thee, Sybil, and thy joys
Are placed in trifles, fashions, follies, toys;
Thou hast sought pleasure in the world around,
That in thine own pure bosom should be found:
Did all that world admire thee, praise and love,
Could it the least of nature's pains remove?
Could it for errors, follies, sins atone,
Or give thee comfort, thoughtful and alone?
It has, believe me, maid, no power to charm   410
Thy soul from sorrow, or thy flesh from harm:
Turn then, fair creature, from a world of sin,
And seek the jewel happiness within.'

'Speak'st thou at meeting?' said the nymph; 'thy speech
Is that of mortal very prone to teach;
But wouldst thou, doctor, from the patient learn
Thine own disease?—The cure is thy concern.'

'Yea, with good will.'—'Then know, 'tis thy complaint,
That, for a sinner, thou'rt too much a saint;
Hast too much show of the sedate and pure,   420

And without cause art formal and demure:
This makes a man unsocial, unpolite;
Odious when wrong, and insolent if right.
Thou may'st be good, but why should goodness be
Wrapt in a garb of such formality?
Thy person well might please a damsel's eye,
In decent habit with a scarlet dye;
But, jest apart—what virtue canst thou trace
In that broad brim that hides thy sober face?
Does that long-skirted drab, that over-nice   430
And formal clothing, prove a scorn of vice?
Then for thine accent—what in sound can be
So void of grace as dull monotony?
Love had a thousand varied notes to move
The human heart;—thou may'st not speak of love
Till thou hast cast thy formal ways aside,
And those becoming youth and nature tried:
Not till exterior freedom, spirit, ease,
Prove it thy study and delight to please;
Not till these follies meet thy just disdain,   440
While yet thy virtues and thy worth remain.'

'This is severe!—Oh! maiden, wilt not thou
Something for habits, manners, modes, allow?'—
'Yes! but allowing much, I much require,
In my behalf, for manner, modes, attire!'

'True, lovely Sybil; and, this point agreed,
Let me to those of greater weight proceed:
Thy father!'—'Nay,' she quickly interposed,
'Good doctor, here our conference is closed!'

Then left the youth, who, lost in his retreat,   450
Pass'd the good matron on her garden-seat;
His looks were troubled, and his air, once mild
And calm, was hurried:—'My audacious child!'
Exclaim'd the dame, 'I read what she has done
In thy displeasure—Ah! the thoughtless one;

94

But yet, Josiah, to my stern good man
Speak of the maid as mildly as you can:
Can you not seem to woo a little while
The daughter's will, the father to beguile?
So that his wrath in time may wear away; 460
Will you preserve our peace, Josiah? say.'

'Yes! my good neighbour,' said the gentle youth,
'Rely securely on my care and truth;
And should thy comfort with my efforts cease,
And only then—perpetual is thy peace.'

The dame had doubts: she well his virtues knew,
His deeds were friendly, and his words were true;
'But to address this vixen is a task
He is ashamed to take, and I to ask.'
Soon as the father from Josiah learn'd 470
What pass'd with Sybil, he the truth discern'd.
'He loves,' the man exclaim'd, 'he loves, 'tis plain,
The thoughtless girl, and shall he love in vain?
She may be stubborn, but she shall be tried,
Born as she is of wilfulness and pride.'

With anger fraught, but willing to persuade,
The wrathful father met the smiling maid:
'Sybil,' said he, 'I long, and yet I dread
To know thy conduct—hath Josiah fled?
And, grieved and fretted by thy scornful air, 480
For his lost peace betaken him to prayer?
Couldst thou his pure and modest mind distress,
By vile remarks upon his speech, address,
Attire, and voice?'—'All this I must confess.'—
'Unhappy child! what labour will it cost
To win him back!'—'I do not think him lost.'—
'Courts he then, trifler! insult and disdain?'—
'No: but from these he courts me to refrain.'—
'Then hear me, Sybil—should Josiah leave
Thy father's house?'—'My father's child would grieve:' 490

'That is of grace, and if he come again
To speak of love?'—'I might from grief refrain.'—
'Then wilt thou, daughter, our design embrace?'—
'Can I resist it, if it be of grace?'
'Dear child! in three plain words thy mind express—
Wilt thou have this good youth?' 'Dear father! yes.'

ARABELLA

OF a fair town where Doctor Rack was guide,
His only daughter was the boast and pride;
Wise Arabella, yet not wise alone,
She like a bright and polish'd brilliant shone;
Her father own'd her for his prop and stay,
Able to guide, yet willing to obey;
Pleased with her learning while discourse could please,
And with her love in languor and disease:
To every mother were her virtues known,
And to their daughters as a pattern shown;   10
Who in her youth had all that age requires,
And with her prudence, all that youth admires:
These odious praises made the damsels try
Not to obtain such merits, but deny;
For, whatsoever wise mammas might say,
To guide a daughter, this was not the way;
From such applause disdain and anger rise,
And envy lives where emulation dies.
In all his strength, contends the noble horse,
With one who just precedes him on the course;   20
But when the rival flies too far before,
His spirit fails, and he attempts no more.

This reasoning maid, above her sex's dread,
Had dared to read, and dared to say she read;
Not the last novel, not the new-born play;
Not the mere trash and scandal of the day;
But (though her young companions felt the shock)
She studied Berkley, Bacon, Hobbes, and Locke:

Her mind within the maze of history dwelt,
And of the moral Muse the beauty felt;   30
The merits of the Roman page she knew,
And could converse with Moore and Montagu:
Thus she became the wonder of the town,
From that she reap'd, to that she gave renown,
And strangers coming, all were taught t' admire
The learned lady, and the lofty spire.

Thus fame in public fix'd the maid, where all
Might throw their darts, and see the idol fall;
A hundred arrows came with vengeance keen,
From tongues envenom'd, and from arms unseen;   40
A thousand eyes were fix'd upon the place,
That, if she fell, she might not fly disgrace:
But malice vainly throws the poison'd dart,
Unless our frailty shows the peccant part;
And Arabella still preserved her name
Untouch'd, and shone with undisputed fame;
Her very notice some respect would cause,
And her esteem was honour and applause.

Men she avoided; not in childish fear,
As if she thought some savage foe was near;   50
Not as a prude, who hides that man should seek,
Or who by silence hints that they should speak;
But with discretion all the sex she view'd,
Ere yet engaged pursuing or pursued;
Ere love had made her to his vices blind,
Or hid the favourite's failings from her mind.

Thus was the picture of the man portray'd,
By merit destined for so rare a maid;
At whose request she might exchange her state,
Or still be happy in a virgin's fate.   60

He must be one with manners like her own,
His life unquestion'd, his opinions known;

G   97

His stainless virtue must all tests endure,
His honour spotless, and his bosom pure;
She no allowance made for sex or times,
Of lax opinion—crimes were ever crimes;
No wretch forsaken must his frailty curse,
No spurious offspring drain his private purse:
He at all times his passions must command,
And yet possess—or be refused her hand.   70

All this without reserve the maiden told,
And some began to weigh the rector's gold;
To ask what sum a prudent man might gain,
Who had such store of virtues to maintain?

A Doctor Campbell, north of Tweed, came forth,
Declared his passion, and proclaim'd his worth;
Not unapproved, for he had much to say
On every cause, and in a pleasant way;
Not all his trust was in a pliant tongue,
His form was good, and ruddy he, and young: 80
But though the doctor was a man of parts,
He read not deeply male or female hearts;
But judged that all whom he esteem'd as wise
Must think alike, though some assumed disguise;
That every reasoning Bramin, Christian, Jew,
Of all religions took their liberal view;
And of her own, no doubt, this learned maid
Denied the substance, and the forms obey'd;
And thus persuaded, he his thoughts express'd
Of her opinions, and his own profess'd: 90
'All states demand this aid, the vulgar need
Their priests and pray'rs, their sermons and their creed;
And those of stronger minds should never speak
(In his opinion) what might hurt the weak:
A man may smile, but still he should attend
His hour at church, and be the church's friend,
What there he thinks conceal, and what he hears com-
        mend.'

Frank was his speech, but heard with high disdain,
Nor had the doctor leave to speak again;
A man who own'd, nay gloried in deceit,   100
'He might despise her, but he should not cheat.'

   The Vicar Holmes appear'd; he heard it said
That ancient men best pleased the prudent maid;
And true it was her ancient friends she loved,
Servants when old she favour'd and approved,
Age in her pious parents she revered,
And neighbours were by length of days endear'd;
But, if her husband too must ancient be,
The good old vicar found it was not he.

   On Captain Bligh her mind in balance hung—   110
Though valiant, modest; and reserved, though young:
Against these merits must defects be set—
Though poor, imprudent; and though proud, in debt:
In vain the captain close attention paid;
She found him wanting, whom she fairly weigh'd.

   Then came a youth, and all their friends agreed,
That Edward Huntly was the man indeed;
Respectful duty he had paid awhile,
Then ask'd her hand, and had a gracious smile:
A lover now declared, he led the fair   120
To woods and fields, to visits and to pray'r;
Then whisper'd softly—'Will you name the day?'
She softly whisper'd—'If you love me, stay:'
'Oh! try me not beyond my strength,' he cried:
'Oh! be not weak,' the prudent maid replied;
'But by some trial your affection prove—
Respect and not impatience argues love:
And love no more is by impatience known,
Than ocean's depth is by its tempests shown:
He whom a weak and fond impatience sways,   130
But for himself with all his fervour prays,
And not the maid he woos, but his own will obeys;

And will she love the being who prefers,
With so much ardour, his desire to hers?'

    Young Edward grieved, but let not grief be seen;
He knew obedience pleased his fancy's queen:
Awhile he waited, and then cried—'Behold!
The year advancing, be no longer cold!'
For she had promised—'Let the flowers appear,
And I will pass with thee the smiling year:'   140
Then pressing grew the youth; the more he press'd,
The less inclined the maid to his request:
'Let June arrive.'—Alas! when April came,
It brought a stranger, and the stranger, shame;
Nor could the lover from his house persuade
A stubborn lass whom he had mournful made;
Angry and weak, by thoughtless vengeance moved,
She told her story to the fair beloved;
In strongest words th' unwelcome truth was shown,
To blight his prospects, careless of her own.   150

    Our heroine grieved, but had too firm a heart
For him to soften, when she swore to part;
In vain his seeming penitence and pray'r,
His vows, his tears; she left him in despair:
His mother fondly laid her grief aside,
And to the reason of the nymph applied—

    'It well becomes thee, lady, to appear,
But not to be, in very truth severe;
Although the crime be odious in thy sight,
That daring sex is taught such things to slight: 160
His heart is thine, although it once was frail;
Think of his grief, and let his love prevail!'—

    'Plead thou no more,' the lofty lass return'd;
'Forgiving woman is deceived and spurn'd:
Say that the crime is common—shall I take
A common man my wedded lord to make?

See! a weak woman by his arts betray'd,
An infant born his father to upbraid;
Shall I forgive his vileness, take his name,
Sanction his error, and partake his shame?   170
No! this assent would kindred frailty prove,
A love for him would be a vicious love:
Can a chaste maiden secret counsel hold
With one whose crime by every mouth is told?
Forbid it, spirit, prudence, virtuous pride;
He must despise me, were he not denied:
The way from vice the erring mind to win
Is with presuming sinners to begin,
And show, by scorning them, a just contempt for sin.'

The youth repulsed, to one more mild convey'd   180
His heart, and smiled on the remorseless maid;
The maid, remorseless in her pride, the while
Despised the insult, and return'd the smile.

First to admire, to praise her, and defend,
Was (now in years advanced) a virgin friend:
Much she preferr'd, she cried, the single state,
'It was her choice'—it surely was her fate;
And much it pleased her in the train to view
A maiden vot'ress, wise and lovely too.

Time to the yielding mind his change imparts,   190
He varies notions, and he alters hearts;
'Tis right, 'tis just to feel contempt for vice,
But he that shows it may be over-nice:
There are who feel, when young, the false sublime,
And proudly love to show disdain for crime;
To whom the future will new thoughts supply,
The pride will soften, and the scorn will die;
Nay, where they still the vice itself condemn,
They bear the vicious, and consort with them:
Young Captain Grove, when one had changed his
    side,   200

Despised the venal turn-coat, and defied;
Old Colonel Grove now shakes him by the hand,
Though he who bribes may still his vote command:
Why would not Ellen to Belinda speak,
When she had flown to London for a week;
And then return'd, to every friend's surprise,
With twice the spirit, and with half the size?
She spoke not then—but after years had flown,
A better friend had Ellen never known:
Was it the lady her mistake had seen?   210
Or had she also such a journey been?
No: 'twas the gradual change in human hearts,
That time, in commerce with the world, imparts;
That on the roughest temper throws disguise,
And steals from virtue her asperities.
The young and ardent, who with glowing zeal
Felt wrath for trifles, and were proud to feel,
Now find those trifles all the mind engage,
To soothe dull hours, and cheat the cares of age;
As young Zelinda, in her quaker-dress,   220
Disdain'd each varying fashion's vile excess,
And now her friends on old Zelinda gaze,
Pleased in rich silks and orient gems to blaze:
Changes like these 'tis folly to condemn,
So virtue yields not, nor is changed with them.

Let us proceed:—Twelve brilliant years were past,
Yet each with less of glory than the last;
Whether these years to this fair virgin gave
A softer mind—effect they often have;
Whether the virgin-state was not so bless'd   230
As that good maiden in her zeal profess'd;
Or whether lovers falling from her train,
Gave greater price to those she could retain,
Is all unknown;—but Arabella now
Was kindly listening to a merchant's vow;
Who offer'd terms so fair, against his love
To strive was folly, so she never strove.—

Man in his earlier days we often find
With a too easy and unguarded mind;
But by increasing years and prudence taught,   240
He grows reserved, and locks up every thought:
Not thus the maiden, for in blooming youth
She hides her thought, and guards the tender truth:
This, when no longer young, no more she hides,
But frankly in the favour'd swain confides:
Man, stubborn man, is like the growing tree,
That longer standing, still will harder be;
And like its fruit, the virgin, first austere,
Then kindly softening with the ripening year.

Now was the lover urgent, and the kind   250
And yielding lady to his suit inclined:
'A little time, my friend, is just, is right;
We must be decent in our neighbours' sight:'
Still she allow'd him of his hopes to speak,
And in compassion took off week by week;
Till few remain'd, when, wearied with delay,
She kindly meant to take off day by day.

That female friend who gave our virgin praise
For flying man and all his treacherous ways,
Now heard with mingled anger, shame, and fear,   260
Of one accepted, and a wedding near;
But she resolved again with friendly zeal
To make the maid her scorn of wedlock feel;
For she was grieved to find her work undone,
And like a sister mourn'd the failing nun.

Why are these gentle maidens prone to make
Their sister-doves the tempting world forsake?
Why all their triumph when a maid disdains
The tyrant-sex, and scorns to wear its chains?
Is it pure joy to see a sister flown   270
From the false pleasures they themselves have known?
Or do they, as the call-birds in the cage,
Try, in pure envy, others to engage;

And therefore paint their native woods and groves,
As scenes of dangerous joys and naughty loves?

Strong was the maiden's hope; her friend was proud,
And had her notions to the world avow'd;
And, could she find the merchant weak and frail,
With power to prove it, then she must prevail;
For she aloud would publish his disgrace,   280
And save his victim from a man so base.

When all inquiries had been duly made,
Came the kind friend her burthen to unlade—
'Alas! my dear! not all our care and art
Can tread the maze of man's deceitful heart:
Look not surprise—nor let resentment swell
Those lovely features, all will yet be well;
And thou, from love's and man's deceptions free,
Wilt dwell in virgin-state, and walk to Heaven with me.'

The maiden frown'd, and then conceived 'that wives   290
Could walk as well, and lead as holy lives
As angry prudes who scorn'd the marriage-chain,
Or luckless maids who sought it still in vain.'

The friend was vex'd—she paused, at length she cried:
'Know your own danger, then your lot decide;
That traitor Beswell, while he seeks your hand,
Has, I affirm, a wanton at command;
A slave, a creature from a foreign place,
The nurse and mother of a spurious race;
Brown, ugly bastards—(Heaven the word forgive,   300
And the deed punish!)—in his cottage live;
To town if business calls him, there he stays
In sinful pleasures wasting countless days;
Nor doubt the facts, for I can witness call
For every crime, and prove them one and all.'

Here ceased th' informer; Arabella's look
Was like a school-boy's puzzled by his book;

Intent she cast her eyes upon the floor,
Paused—then replied—
      'I wish to know no more:
I question not your motive, zeal, or love,   310
But much decline such dubious points to prove—
All is not true, I judge, for who can guess
Those deeds of darkness men with care suppress?
He brought a slave perhaps to England's coast,
And made her free; it is our country's boast!
And she perchance too grateful—good and ill
Were sown at first, and grow together still;
The colour'd infants on the village-green,
What are they more than we have often seen?
Children half-clothed who round their village stray, 320
In sun or rain, now starved, now beaten, they
Will the dark colour of their fate betray:
Let us in Christian love for all account,
And then behold to what such tales amount.'

'His heart is evil,' said th' impatient friend:
'My duty bids me try that heart to mend,'
Replied the virgin—'We may be too nice,
And lose a soul in our contempt of vice;
If false the charge, I then shall show regard
For a good man, and be his just reward: 330
And what for virtue can I better do
Than to reclaim him, if the charge be true?'

She spoke, nor more her holy work delay'd;
'Twas time to lend an erring mortal aid:
'The noblest way,' she judged, 'a soul to win,
Was with an act of kindness to begin,
To make the sinner sure, and then t' attack the sin.' [1]

[1] As the author's purpose in this Tale may be mistaken, he wishes to observe, that conduct like that of the lady's here described must be meritorious or censurable just as the motives to it are pure or selfish; that these motives may in a great measure be concealed from the mind of the agent; and that we often take credit to our virtue for actions which spring originally from our tempers, inclinations, or our indifference. It cannot therefore be improper, much less immoral, to give an instance of such self-deception.

THE LOVER'S JOURNEY

IT is the soul that sees; the outward eyes
Present the object, but the mind descries;
And thence delight, disgust, or cool indiff'rence rise:
When minds are joyful, then we look around,
And what is seen is all on fairy ground;
Again they sicken, and on every view
Cast their own dull and melancholy hue;
Or, if absorb'd by their peculiar cares,
The vacant eye on viewless matter glares,
Our feelings still upon our views attend,   10
And their own natures to the objects lend;
Sorrow and joy are in their influence sure,
Long as the passion reigns th' effects endure;
But love in minds his various changes makes,
And clothes each object with the change he takes;
His light and shade on every view he throws,
And on each object, what he feels, bestows.

Fair was the morning, and the month was June,
When rose a lover; love awakens soon;
Brief his repose, yet much he dreamt the while   20
Of that day's meeting, and his Laura's smile;
Fancy and love that name assign'd to her,
Call'd Susan in the parish-register;
And he no more was John—his Laura gave
The name Orlando to her faithful slave.

Bright shone the glory of the rising day,
When the fond traveller took his favourite way;
He mounted gaily, felt his bosom light,
And all he saw was pleasing in his sight.

'Ye hours of expectation, quickly fly,   30
And bring on hours of blest reality;
When I shall Laura see, beside her stand,
Hear her sweet voice, and press her yielded hand.'

First o'er a barren heath beside the coast
Orlando rode, and joy began to boast.

'This neat low gorse,' said he, 'with golden bloom,
Delights each sense, is beauty, is perfume;
And this gay ling, with all its purple flowers,
A man at leisure might admire for hours;
This green-fringed cup-moss has a scarlet tip,   40
That yields to nothing but my Laura's lip ;
And then how fine this herbage! men may say
A heath is barren; nothing is so gay:
Barren or bare to call such charming scene
Argues a mind possess'd by care and spleen.'

Onward he went, and fiercer grew the heat,
Dust rose in clouds before the horse's feet;
For now he pass'd through lanes of burning sand,
Bounds to thin crops or yet uncultured land;
Where the dark poppy flourished on the dry   50
And sterile soil, and mock'd the thin-set rye.

'How lovely this!' the rapt Orlando said;
With what delight is labouring man repaid!
The very lane has sweets that all admire,
The rambling suckling and the vigorous brier;
See! wholesome wormwood grows beside the way,
Where dew-press'd yet the dog-rose bends the spray;
Fresh herbs the fields, fair shrubs the banks adorn,
And snow-white bloom falls flaky from the thorn;
No fostering hand they need, no sheltering wall,   60
They spring uncultured, and they bloom for all.'

The lover rode as hasty lovers ride,
And reach'd a common pasture wild and wide;
Small black-legg'd sheep devour with hunger keen
The meagre herbage, fleshless, lank, and lean;
Such o'er thy level turf, Newmarket! stray,
And there, with other *black-legs* find their prey:

He saw some scatter'd hovels; turf was piled
In square brown stacks; a prospect bleak and wild!
A mill, indeed, was in the centre found,   70
With short sear herbage withering all around;
A smith's black shed opposed a wright's long shop,
And join'd an inn where humble travellers stop.

'Ay, this is Nature,' said the gentle 'squire;
'This ease, peace, pleasure—who would not admire?
With what delight these sturdy children play,
And joyful rustics at the close of day;
Sport follows labour, on this even space
Will soon commence the wrestling and the race;
Then will the village-maidens leave their home,   80
And to the dance with buoyant spirits come;
No affectation in their looks is seen,
Nor know they what disguise or flattery mean;
Nor aught to move an envious pang they see,
Easy their service, and their love is free;
Hence early springs that love, it long endures,
And life's first comfort, while they live, ensures:
They the low roof and rustic comforts prize,
Nor cast on prouder mansions envying eyes:
Sometimes the news at yonder town they hear,   90
And learn what busier mortals feel and fear;
Secure themselves, although by tales amazed,
Of towns bombarded and of cities razed;
As if they doubted, in their still retreat,
The very news that makes their quiet sweet,
And their days happy—happier only knows
He on whom Laura her regard bestows.'

On rode Orlando, counting all the while
The miles he pass'd and every coming mile;
Like all attracted things, he quicker flies,   100
The place approaching where th' attraction lies;
When next appear'd a *dam*—so call the place—
Where lies a road confined in narrow space;

A work of labour, for on either side
Is level fen, a prospect wild and wide,
With dikes on either hand by ocean's self supplied:
Far on the right the distant sea is seen,
And salt the springs that feed the marsh between;
Beneath an ancient bridge, the straiten'd flood
Rolls through its sloping banks of slimy mud;   110
Near it a sunken boat resists the tide,
That frets and hurries to th' opposing side;
The rushes sharp, that on the borders grow,
Bend their brown flow'rets to the stream below,
Impure in all its course, in all its progress slow:
Here a grave Flora scarcely deigns to bloom,
Nor wears a rosy blush, nor sheds perfume;
The few dull flowers that o'er the place are spread
Partake the nature of their fenny bed;
Here on its wiry stem, in rigid bloom,   120
Grows the salt lavender that lacks perfume;
Here the dwarf sallows creep, the septfoil harsh,
And the soft slimy mallow of the marsh;
Low on the ear the distant billows sound,
And just in view appears their stony bound;
No hedge nor tree conceals the glowing sun,
Birds, save a wat'ry tribe, the district shun,
Nor chirp among the reeds where bitter waters run.

'Various as beauteous, Nature, is thy face,'
Exclaim'd Orlando: 'all that grows has grace;   130
All are appropriate—bog, and marsh and fen,
Are only poor to undiscerning men;
Here may the nice and curious eye explore
How Nature's hand adorns the rushy moor;
Here the rare moss in secret shade is found,
Here the sweet myrtle of the shaking ground;
Beauties are these that from the view retire,
But well repay th' attention they require;
For these my Laura will her home forsake,
And all the pleasures they afford partake.'   140

Again the country was enclosed, a wide
And sandy road has banks on either side;
Where lo! a hollow on the left appear'd,
And there a gipsy-tribe their tent had rear'd;
'Twas open spread, to catch the morning sun,
And they had now their early meal begun,
When two brown boys just left their grassy seat,
The early trav'ller with their pray'rs to greet:
While yet Orlando held his pence in hand,
He saw their sister on her duty stand;   150
Some twelve years old, demure, affected, sly,
Prepared the force of early powers to try;
Sudden a look of languor he descries,
And well-feign'd apprehension in her eyes;
Train'd but yet savage, in her speaking face
He mark'd the features of her vagrant race;
When a light laugh and roguish leer express'd
The vice implanted in her youthful breast:
Forth from the tent her elder brother came,
Who seem'd offended, yet forbore to blame   160
The young designer, but could only trace
The looks of pity in the trav'ller's face:
Within, the father, who from fences nigh
Had brought the fuel for the fire's supply,
Watch'd now the feeble blaze, and stood dejected by:
On ragged rug, just borrow'd from the bed,
And by the hand of coarse indulgence fed,
In dirty patchwork negligently dress'd,
Reclined the wife, an infant at her breast;
In her wild face some touch of grace remain'd,   170
Of vigour palsied and of beauty stain'd;
Her blood-shot eyes on her unheeding mate
Were wrathful turn'd, and seem'd her wants to state,
Cursing his tardy aid—her mother there
With gipsy-state engross'd the only chair;
Solemn and dull her look; with such she stands,
And reads the milk-maid's fortune in her hands,
Tracing the lines of life; assumed through years,

Each feature now the steady falsehood wears;
With hard and savage eye she views the food,   180
And grudging pinches their intruding brood;
Last in the group, the worn-out grandsire sits
Neglected, lost, and living but by fits;
Useless, despised, his worthless labours done,
And half protected by the vicious son,
Who half supports him; he with heavy glance
Views the young ruffians who around him dance;
And, by the sadness in his face, appears
To trace the progress of their future years:
Through what strange course of misery, vice, deceit,   190
Must wildly wander each unpractised cheat!
What shame and grief, what punishment and pain,
Sport of fierce passions, must each child sustain—
Ere they like him approach their latter end,
Without a hope, a comfort, or a friend!

But this Orlando felt not; 'Rogues,' said he,
'Doubtless they are, but merry rogues they be;
They wander round the land, and be it true,
They break the laws—then let the laws pursue
The wanton idlers; for the life they live,   200
Acquit I cannot, but I can forgive.'
This said, a portion from his purse was thrown,
And every heart seem'd happy like his own.

He hurried forth, for now the town was nigh—
'The happiest man of mortal men am I.'
Thou art! but change in every state is near,
(So while the wretched hope, the blest may fear);
'Say, where is Laura?'—'That her words must show,'
A lass replied; 'read this, and thou shalt know!'

'What, gone!'—her friend insisted—forced to go:—   210
'Is vex'd, was teased, could not refuse her!—No?'
'But you can follow:' 'Yes:' 'The miles are few,
The way is pleasant; will you come?—Adieu!

Thy Laura!' 'No! I feel I must resign
The pleasing hope, thou hadst been here, if mine:
A lady was it?—Was no brother there?
But why should I afflict me if there were?'
'The way is pleasant:' 'What to me the way?
I cannot reach her till the close of day.
My dumb companion! is it thus we speed?   220
Not I from grief nor thou from toil art freed;
Still art thou doom'd to travel and to pine,
For my vexation—What a fate is mine!

'Gone to a friend, she tells me; I commend
Her purpose; means she to a female friend?
By Heaven, I wish she suffer'd half the pain
Of hope protracted through the day in vain:
Shall I persist to see th' ungrateful maid?
Yes, I will see her, slight her, and upbraid:
What! in the very hour? She knew the time,   230
And doubtless chose it to increase her crime.'

Forth rode Orlando by a river's side,
Inland and winding, smooth, and full and wide,
That roll'd majestic on, in one soft-flowing tide;
The bottom gravel, flow'ry were the banks,
Tall willows, waving in their broken ranks;
The road, now near, now distant, winding led
By lovely meadows which the waters fed;
He pass'd the way-side inn, the village spire,
Nor stopp'd to gaze, to question, or admire;   240
On either side the rural mansions stood,
With hedge-row trees, and hills high-crown'd with wood,
And many a devious stream that reach'd the nobler flood.

'I hate these scenes,' Orlando angry cried,
'And these proud farmers! yes, I hate their pride:
See! that sleek fellow, how he strides along,
Strong as an ox, and ignorant as strong;
Can yon close crops a single eye detain

But his who counts the profits of the grain?
And these vile beans with deleterious smell,   250
Where is their beauty? can a mortal tell?
These deep fat meadows I detest; it shocks
One's feelings there to see the grazing ox;—
For slaughter fatted, as a lady's smile
Rejoices man, and means his death the while.
Lo! now the sons of labour! every day
Employ'd in toil, and vex'd in every way;
Theirs is but mirth assumed, and they conceal,
In their affected joys, the ills they feel:
I hate these long green lanes; there's nothing seen   260
In this vile country but eternal green;
Woods! waters! meadows! Will they never end?
'Tis a vile prospect:—Gone to see a friend!'

Still on he rode! a mansion fair and tall
Rose on his view—the pride of Loddon-hall:
Spread o'er the park he saw the grazing steer,
The full-fed steed, the herds of bounding deer:
On a clear stream the vivid sunbeams play'd,
Through noble elms, and on the surface made
That moving picture, checker'd light and shade;   270
Th' attended children, there indulged to stray,
Enjoy'd and gave new beauty to the day;
Whose happy parents from their room were seen
Pleased with the sportive idlers on the green.

'Well!' said Orlando, 'and for one so bless'd,
A thousand reasoning wretches are distress'd;
Nay, these so seeming glad, are grieving like the rest:
Man is a cheat—and all but strive to hide
Their inward misery by their outward pride.
What do yon lofty gates and walls contain,   280
But fruitless means to soothe unconquer'd pain?
The parents read each infant daughter's smile,
Form'd to seduce, encouraged to beguile;
They view the boys unconscious of their fate,

Sure to be tempted, sure to take the bait;
These will be Lauras, sad Orlandos these—
There's guilt and grief in all one hears and sees.'

Our trav'ller, lab'ring up a hill, look'd down
Upon a lively, busy, pleasant town;
All he beheld were there alert, alive,   290
The busiest bees that ever stock'd a hive:
A pair were married, and the bells aloud
Proclaim'd their joy, and joyful seem'd the crowd;
And now proceeding on his way, he spied,
Bound by strong ties, the bridegroom and the bride;
Each by some friends attended, near they drew,
And spleen beheld them with prophetic view.

'Married! nay, mad!' Orlando cried in scorn;
'Another wretch on this unlucky morn:
What are this foolish mirth, these idle joys?   300
Attempts to stifle doubt and fear by noise:
To me these robes, expressive of delight,
Foreshow distress, and only grief excite;
And for these cheerful friends, will they behold
Their wailing brood in sickness, want, and cold;
And his proud look, and her soft languid air
Will—but I spare you—go, unhappy pair!'

And now approaching to the journey's end,
His anger fails, his thoughts to kindness tend,
He less offended feels, and rather fears t' offend: 310
Now gently rising, hope contends with doubt,
And casts a sunshine on the views without;
And still reviving joy and lingering gloom
Alternate empire o'er his soul assume;
Till, long perplex'd, he now began to find
The softer thoughts engross the settling mind:
He saw the mansion, and should quickly see
His Laura's self—and angry could he be?
No! the resentment melted all away—

'For this my grief a single smile will pay,'   320
Our trav'ller cried;—'And why should it offend,
That one so good should have a pressing friend?
Grieve not, my heart! to find a favourite guest
Thy pride and boast—ye selfish sorrows, rest;
She will be kind, and I again be blest.'

While gentler passions thus his bosom sway'd,
He reach'd the mansion, and he saw the maid;
'My Laura!'—'My Orlando!—this is kind;
In truth I came persuaded, not inclined:
Our friends' amusement let us now pursue,   330
And I to-morrow will return with you.'

Like man entranced, the happy lover stood—
'As Laura wills, for she is kind and good;
Ever the truest, gentlest, fairest, best—
As Laura wills, I see her and am blest.'

Home went the lovers through that busy place,
By Loddon-Hall, the country's pride and grace;
By the rich meadows where the oxen fed,
Through the green vale that form'd the river's bed;
And by unnumber'd cottages and farms,   340
That have for musing minds unnumber'd charms;
And how affected by the view of these
Was then Orlando—did they pain or please?

Nor pain nor pleasure could they yield—and why?
The mind was fill'd, was happy, and the eye
Roved o'er the fleeting views, that but appear'd to die.

Alone Orlando on the morrow paced
The well-known road; the gipsy-tent he traced;
The dam high-raised, the reedy dykes between,
The scatter'd hovels on the barren green,   350
The burning sand, the fields of thin-set rye,
Mock'd by the useless Flora, blooming by;

And last the heath with all its various bloom,
And the close lanes that led the trav'ller home.

Then could these scenes the former joys renew?
Or was there now dejection in the view?—
Nor one or other would they yield—and why?
The mind was absent, and the vacant eye
Wander'd o'er viewless scenes, that but appear'd to die.

ADVICE; or, THE 'SQUIRE AND THE PRIEST

A WEALTHY lord of far-extended land
Had all that pleased him placed at his command;
Widow'd of late, but finding much relief
In the world's comforts, he dismiss'd his grief;
He was by marriage of his daughters eased,
And knew his sons could marry if they pleased;
Meantime in travel he indulged the boys,
And kept no spy nor partner of his joys.

These joys, indeed, were of the grosser kind,
That fed the cravings of an earthly mind;   10
A mind that, conscious of its own excess,
Felt the reproach his neighbours would express.
Long at th' indulgent board he loved to sit,
Where joy was laughter, and profaneness wit;
And such the guest and manners of the hall,
No wedded lady on the 'Squire would call:
Here reign'd a favourite, and her triumph gain'd
O'er other favourites who before had reign'd;
Reserved and modest seem'd the nymph to be,
Knowing her lord was charm'd with modesty;   20
For he, a sportsman keen, the more enjoy'd,
The greater value had the thing destroy'd.

Our 'Squire declared, that, from a wife released,
He would no more give trouble to a priest;

Seem'd it not, then, ungrateful and unkind,
That he should trouble from the priesthood find?
The church he honour'd, and he gave the due
And full respect to every son he knew;
But envied those who had the luck to meet
A gentle pastor, civil, and discreet;   30
Who never bold and hostile sermon penn'd,
To wound a sinner, or to shame a friend;
One whom no being either shunn'd or fear'd,
Such must be loved wherever they appear'd.

Not such the stern old rector of the time,
Who soothed no culprit, and who spared no crime;
Who would his fears and his contempt express,
For irreligion and licentiousness;
Of him our village lord, his guests among,
By speech vindictive proved his feelings stung.   40

'Were he a bigot,' said the 'Squire, 'whose zeal
Condemn'd us all, I should disdain to feel:
But when a man of parts in college train'd,
Prates of our conduct—who would not be pain'd?
While he declaims (where no one dares reply)
On men abandon'd, grov'ling in the sty
(Like beasts in human shape) of shameless luxury.
Yet with a patriot's zeal I stand the shock
Of vile rebuke, example to his flock:
But let this rector, thus severe and proud,   50
Change his wide surplice for a narrow shroud,
And I will place within his seat a youth,
Train'd by the graces, to explain the truth;
Then shall the flock with gentle hand be led,
By wisdom won, and by compassion fed.'

This purposed teacher was a sister's son,
Who of her children gave the priesthood one;
And she had early train'd for this employ
The pliant talents of her college boy:

At various times her letters painted all   60
Her brother's views—the manners of the hall;
The rector's harshness, and the mischief made
By chiding those whom preachers should persuade:
This led the youth to views of easy life,
A friendly patron, an obliging wife;
His tithe, his glebe, the garden and the steed,
With books as many as he wish'd to read.

All this accorded with the uncle's will;
He loved a priest compliant, easy, still;
Sums he had often to his favourite sent,   70
'To be,' he wrote, 'in manly freedom spent;
For well it pleased his spirit to assist
An honest lad, who scorn'd a Methodist:'
His mother too, in her maternal care,
Bade him of canting hypocrites beware;
Who from his duties would his heart seduce,
And make his talents of no earthly use.

Soon must a trial of his worth be made—
The ancient priest is to the tomb convey'd;
And the youth summon'd from a serious friend,   80
His guide and host, new duties to attend.

Three months before, the nephew and the 'Squire
Saw mutual worth to praise and to admire;
And though the one too early left his wine,
The other still exclaim'd—'My boy will shine:
Yes, I perceive that he will soon improve,
And I shall form the very guide I love;
Decent abroad, he will my name defend,
And, when at home, be social and unbend.'

The plan was specious, for the mind of James   90
Accorded duly with his uncle's schemes:
He then aspired not to a higher name

Than sober clerks of moderate talents claim;
Gravely to pray, and rev'rendly to preach,
Was all he saw, good youth! within his reach:
Thus may a mass of sulphur long abide,
Cold and inert, but, to the flame applied,
Kindling it blazes, and consuming turns
To smoke and poison, as it boils and burns.

James, leaving college, to a preacher stray'd;   100
What call'd he knew not—but the call obey'd:
Mild, idle, pensive, ever led by those
Who could some specious novelty propose;
Humbly he listen'd, while the preacher dwelt
On touching themes, and strong emotions felt;
And in this night was fix'd that pliant will
To one sole point, and he retains it still.

At first his care was to himself confined;
Himself assured, he gave it to mankind:
His zeal grew active—honest, earnest zeal,   110
And comfort dealt to him, he long'd to deal;
He to his favourite preacher now withdrew,
Was taught to teach, instructed to subdue;
And train'd for ghostly warfare, when the call
Of his new duties reach'd him from the hall.

Now to the 'Squire, although alert and stout,
Came unexpected an attack of gout;
And the grieved patron felt such serious pain,
He never thought to see a church again:
Thrice had the youthful rector taught the crowd,   120
Whose growing numbers spoke his powers aloud,
Before the patron could himself rejoice
(His pain still lingering) in the general voice;
For he imputed all this early fame
To graceful manner, and the well-known name;
And to himself assumed a share of praise,
For worth and talents he was pleased to raise.

A month had flown, and with it fled disease;
What pleased before, began again to please:
Emerging daily from his chamber's gloom,   130
He found his old sensations hurrying home;
Then call'd his nephew, and exclaim'd, 'My boy,
Let us again the balm of life enjoy;
The foe has left me, and I deem it right,
Should he return, to arm me for the fight.'

Thus spoke the 'Squire, the favourite nymph stood by,
And view'd the priest with insult in her eye:
She thrice had heard him when he boldly spoke
On dangerous points, and fear'd he would revoke:
For James she loved not—and her manner told,   140
'This warm affection will be quickly cold:'
And still she fear'd impression might be made
Upon a subject, nervous and decay'd;
She knew her danger, and had no desire
Of reformation in the gallant 'Squire;
And felt an envious pleasure in her breast
To see the rector daunted and distress'd.

Again the uncle to the youth applied—
'Cast, my dear lad, that cursed gloom aside:
There are for all things time and place; appear   150
Grave in your pulpit, and be merry here:
Now take your wine—for woes a sure resource,
And the best prelude to a long discourse.'

James half obey'd, but cast an angry eye
On the fair lass, who still stood watchful by;
Resolving thus, 'I have my fears—but still
I must perform my duties, and I will;
No love, no interest, shall my mind control;
Better to lose my comforts than my soul;
Better my uncle's favour to abjure,   160
Than the upbraidings of my heart endure.'

He took his glass, and then address'd the 'Squire:
'I feel not well, permit me to retire.'
The 'Squire conceived that the ensuing day
Gave him these terrors for the grand essay,
When he himself should this young preacher try,
And stand before him with observant eye;
This raised compassion in his manly breast,
And he would send the rector to his rest:
Yet first, in soothing voice—'A moment stay,   170
And these suggestions of a friend obey;
Treasure these hints, if fame or peace you prize—
The bottle emptied, I shall close my eyes.

'On every priest a two-fold care attends,
To prove his talents, and insure his friends:
First, of the first—your stores at once produce,
And bring your reading to its proper use:
On doctrines dwell, and every point enforce
By quoting much, the scholar's sure resource;
For he alone can show us on each head   180
What ancient schoolmen and sage fathers said:
No worth has knowledge, if you fail to show
How well you studied and how much you know:
Is faith your subject, and you judge it right
On theme so dark to cast a ray of light;
Be it that faith the orthodox maintain,
Found in the rubric, what the creeds explain;
Fail not to show us on this ancient faith
(And quote the passage) what some martyr saith:
Dwell not one moment on a faith that shocks   190
The minds of men sincere and orthodox;
That gloomy faith, that robs the wounded mind
Of all the comfort it was wont to find
From virtuous acts, and to the soul denies
Its proper due for alms and charities;
That partial faith, that, weighing sins alone,
Lets not a virtue for a fault atone;
That starving faith, that would our tables clear,

And make one dreadful Lent of all the year;
And cruel too, for this is faith that rends   200
Confiding beauties from protecting friends;
A faith that all embracing, what a gloom
Deep and terrific o'er the land would come!
What scenes of horror would that time disclose!
No sight but misery, and no sound but woes;
Your nobler faith, in loftier style convey'd,
Shall be with praise and admiration paid:
On points like these your hearers all admire
A preacher's depth, and nothing more require;
Shall we a studious youth to college send,   210
That every clown his words may comprehend?
'Tis for your glory, when your hearers own
Your learning matchless, but the sense unknown.

'Thus honour gain'd, learn how to gain a friend,
And the sure way is—never to offend;
For, James, consider—what your neighbours do
Is their own business, and concerns not you:
Shun all resemblance to that forward race
Who preach of sins before a sinner's face;
And seem as if they overlook'd a pew,   220
Only to drag a failing man in view:
Much should I feel, when groaning in disease,
If a rough hand upon my limb should seize;
But great my anger, if this hand were found
The very doctor's who should make it sound:
So feel our minds, young priest, so doubly feel,
When hurt by those whose office is to heal.

'Yet of our duties you must something tell,
And must at times on sin and frailty dwell;
Here you may preach in easy, flowing style,   230
How errors cloud us, and how sins defile:
Here bring persuasive tropes and figures forth,
To show the poor that wealth is nothing worth;
That they, in fact, possess an ample share

122

Of the world's good, and feel not half its care;
Give them this comfort, and, indeed, my gout
In its full vigour causes me some doubt;
And let it always, for your zeal, suffice,
That vice you combat, in the abstract—vice:
The very captious will be quiet then;   240
We all confess we are offending men:
In lashing sin, of every stroke beware,
For sinners feel, and sinners you must spare;
In general satire, every man perceives
A slight attack, yet neither fears nor grieves;
But name th' offence, and you absolve the rest,
And point the dagger at a single breast.

'Yet are there sinners of a class so low,
That you with safety may the lash bestow;
Poachers, and drunkards, idle rogues, who feed   250
At others' cost, a mark'd correction need:
And all the better sort, who see your zeal,
Will love and reverence for their pastor feel;
Reverence for one who can inflict the smart,
And love, because he deals them not a part.

'Remember well what love and age advise;
A quiet rector is a parish prize,
Who in his learning has a decent pride;
Who to his people is a gentle guide;
Who only hints at failings that he sees;   260
Who loves his glebe, his patron, and his ease,
And finds the way to fame and profit is to please.'

The nephew answer'd not, except a sigh
And look of sorrow might be term'd reply;
He saw the fearful hazard of his state,
And held with truth and safety strong debate;
Nor long he reason'd, for the zealous youth
Resolved, though timid, to profess the truth;

And though his friend should like a lion roar,
Truth would he preach, and neither less nor more.   270

The bells had toll'd—arrived the time of prayer,
The flock assembled, and the 'Squire was there:
And now can poet sing, or proseman say,
The disappointment of that trying day?

As he who long had train'd a favourite steed,
(Whose blood and bone gave promise of his speed),
Sanguine with hope, he runs with partial eye
O'er every feature, and his bets are high;
Of triumph sure, he sees the rivals start,
And waits their coming with exulting heart;   280
Forestalling glory, with impatient glance,
And sure to see his conquering steed advance;
The conquering steed advances—luckless day!
A rival's Herod bears the prize away,
Nor second his, nor third, but lagging last,
With hanging head he comes, by all surpass'd:
Surprise and wrath the owner's mind inflame,
Love turns to scorn, and glory ends in shame;—
Thus waited, high in hope, the partial 'Squire,
Eager to hear, impatient to admire: 290
When the young preacher in the tones that find
A certain passage to the kindling mind,
With air and accent strange, impressive, sad,
Alarm'd the judge—he trembled for the lad;
But when the text announced the power of grace,
Amazement scowl'd upon his clouded face,
At this degenerate son of his illustrious race;
Staring he stood, till hope again arose,
That James might well define the words he chose:
For this he listen'd—but, alas! he found   300
The preacher always on forbidden ground.

And now the uncle left the hated pew,
With James, and James's conduct in his view:

A long farewell to all his favourite schemes!
For now no crazed fanatic's frantic dreams
Seem'd vile as James's conduct, or as James:
All he had long derided, hated, fear'd,
This, from the chosen youth the uncle heard;—
The needless pause, the fierce disorder'd air,
The groan for sin, the vehemence of prayer,   310
Gave birth to wrath, that, in a long discourse
Of grace, triumphant, rose to four-fold force:
He found his thoughts despised, his rules transgress'd,
And while the anger kindled in his breast,
The pain must be endured that could not be express'd:
Each new idea more inflamed his ire,
As fuel thrown upon a rising fire:
A hearer yet, he sought by threatening sign
To ease his heart, and awe the young divine;
But James refused those angry looks to meet,   320
Till he dismiss'd his flock, and left his seat:
Exhausted then he felt his trembling frame,
But fix'd his soul—his sentiments the same;
And therefore wise it seem'd to fly from rage,
And seek for shelter in his parsonage:
There, if forsaken, yet consoled to find
Some comforts left, though not a few resign'd;
There, if he lost an erring parent's love,
An honest conscience must the cause approve;
If the nice palate were no longer fed,   330
The mind enjoy'd delicious thoughts instead;
And if some part of earthly good was flown,
Still was the tithe of ten good farms his own.

Fear now, and discord, in the village reign,
The cool remonstrate, and the meek complain;
But there is war within, and wisdom pleads in vain:
Now dreads the uncle, and proclaims his dread,
Lest the boy-priest should turn each rustic head;
The certain converts cost him certain wo,
The doubtful fear lest they should join the foe: 340

Matrons of old, with whom he used to joke,
Now pass his Honour with a pious look;
Lasses, who met him once with lively airs,
Now cross his way, and gravely walk to prayers:
An old companion, whom he long has loved,
By coward fears confess'd his conscience moved;
As the third bottle gave its spirit forth,
And they bore witness to departed worth,
The friend arose, and he too would depart:—
'Man,' said the 'Squire, 'thou wert not wont to start; 350
Hast thou attended to that foolish boy,
Who would abridge all comforts, or destroy?'

Yes, he had listen'd, who had slumber'd long,
And was convinced that something must be wrong:
But, though affected, still his yielding heart,
And craving palate, took the uncle's part;
Wine now oppress'd him, who, when free from wine,
Could seldom clearly utter his design;
But though by nature and indulgence weak,
Yet, half converted, he resolved to speak; 360
And, speaking, own'd, 'that in his mind the youth
Had gifts and learning, and that truth was truth:
The 'Squire he honour'd, and, for his poor part,
He hated nothing like a hollow heart:
But 'twas a maxim he had often tried,
That right was right, and there he would abide;
He honour'd learning, and he would confess
The preacher had his talents—more or less:
Why not agree? he thought the young divine
Had no such strictness—they might drink and dine; 370
For them sufficient—but he said before,—
That truth was truth, and he would drink no more.'

This heard the 'Squire with mix'd contempt and pain;
He fear'd the priest this recreant sot would gain.
The favourite nymph, though not a convert made,
Conceived the man she scorn'd her cause would aid;

And when the spirits of her lord were low,
The lass presumed the wicked cause to show:
'It was the wretched life his Honour led,
And would draw vengeance on his guilty head; 380
Their loves (Heav'n knew how dreadfully distress'd
The thought had made her!) were as yet unbless'd:
And till the church had sanction'd'——Here she saw
The wrath that forced her trembling to withdraw.

Add to these outward ills, some inward light,
That show'd him all was not correct and right:
Though now he less indulged—and to the poor,
From day to day, sent alms from door to door;
Though he some ease from easy virtues found,
Yet conscience told him he could not compound; 390
But must himself the darling sin deny,
Change the whole heart—but here a heavy sigh
Proclaim'd, 'How vast the toil! and ah! how weak am I!'

James too has trouble—he divided sees
A parish, once harmonious and at ease:
With him united are the simply meek,
The warm, the sad, the nervous, and the weak;
The rest his uncle's, save the few beside,
Who own no doctrine, and obey no guide;
With stragglers of each adverse camp, who lend 400
Their aid to both, but each in turn offend.

Though zealous still, yet he begins to feel
The heat too fierce, that glows in vulgar zeal;
With pain he hears his simple friends relate
Their week's experience, and their woful state:
With small temptation struggling every hour,
And bravely battling with the tempting power;
His native sense is hurt by strange complaints
Of inward motions in these warring saints;
Who never cast on sinful bait a look, 410
But they perceive the devil at the hook:

Grieved, yet compell'd to smile, he finds it hard
Against the blunders of conceit to guard;
He sighs to hear the jests his converts cause,
He cannot give their erring zeal applause;
But finds it inconsistent to condemn
The flights and follies he has nursed in them:
These, in opposing minds, contempt produce,
Or mirth occasion, or provoke abuse;
On each momentous theme disgrace they bring,   420
And give to Scorn her poison and her sting.

THE WAGER

'Tis thought your deer doth hold you at a bay.
                    Taming the Shrew, Act II. Scene 1.

———

I choose her for myself;
If she and I are pleased, what's that to you?
                    ———, Act V. Scene 2.

———

Let's send each one to his wife,
And he whose wife is most obedient
Shall win the wager.
                    ———, Act V. Scene 2.

———

Now by the world it is a lusty wench,
I love her ten times more than e'er I did.
                    ———, Act II. Scene 1.

COUNTER and Clubb were men in trade, whose pains,
Credit, and prudence, brought them constant gains;
Partners and punctual, every friend agreed
Counter and Clubb were men who must succeed.
When they had fix'd some little time in life,
Each thought of taking to himself a wife:
As men in trade alike, as men in love
They seem'd with no according views to move;

128

As certain ores in outward view the same,
They show'd their difference when the magnet came. 10
Counter was vain: with spirit strong and high,
'Twas not in him like suppliant swain to sigh:
'His wife might o'er his men and maids preside,
And in her province be a judge and guide;
But what he thought, or did, or wish'd to do,
She must not know, or censure if she knew;
At home, abroad, by day, by night, if he
On aught determined, so it was to be:
How is a man,' he ask'd, 'for business fit,
Who to a female can his will submit? 20
Absent awhile, let no inquiring eye
Or plainer speech presume to question why:
But all be silent; and, when seen again,
Let all be cheerful—shall a wife complain?
Friends I invite, and who shall dare t' object,
Or look on them with coolness or neglect?
No! I must ever of my house be head,
And, thus obey'd, I condescend to wed.'

Clubb heard the speech—'My friend is nice,' said he;
'A wife with less respect will do for me: 30
How is he certain such a prize to gain?
What he approves, a lass may learn to feign,
And so affect t' obey till she begins to reign;
Awhile complying, she may vary then,
And be as wives of more unwary men;
Beside, to him who plays such lordly part,
How shall a tender creature yield her heart?
Should he the promised confidence refuse,
She may another more confiding choose;
May show her anger, yet her purpose hide, 40
And wake his jealousy, and wound his pride.
In one so humbled, who can trace the friend?
I on an equal, not a slave, depend;
If true, my confidence is wisely placed,
And being false, she only is disgraced.'

I   129

Clubb, with these notions, cast his eye around,
And one so easy soon a partner found.
The lady chosen was of good repute;
Meekness she had not, and was seldom mute;
Though quick to anger, still she loved to smile;   50
And would be calm if men would wait a while:
She knew her duty, and she loved her way,
More pleased in truth to govern than obey;
She heard her priest with reverence, and her spouse
As one who felt the pressure of her vows;
Useful and civil, all her friends confess'd—
Give her her way, and she would choose the best;
Though some indeed a sly remark would make—
Give it her not, and she would choose to take.

All this, when Clubb some cheerful months had 60
He saw, confess'd, and said he was content.   [spent,

Counter meantime selected, doubted, weigh'd,
And then brought home a young complying maid;—
A tender creature, full of fears as charms,
A beauteous nursling from its mother's arms;
A soft, sweet blossom, such as men must love,
But to preserve must keep it in the stove:
She had a mild, subdued, expiring look—
Raise but the voice, and this fair creature shook;
Leave her alone, she felt a thousand fears—   70
Chide, and she melted into floods of tears;
Fondly she pleaded and would gently sigh,
For very pity, or she knew not why;
One whom to govern none could be afraid—
Hold up the finger, this meek thing obey'd;
Her happy husband had the easiest task—
Say but his will, no question would she ask;
She sought no reasons, no affairs she knew,
Of business spoke not, and had nought to do.

Oft he exclaim'd, 'How meek! how mild! how kind! 80
With her 'twere cruel but to seem unkind;

Though ever silent when I take my leave,
It pains my heart to think how hers will grieve;
'Tis heaven on earth with such a wife to dwell,
I am in raptures to have sped so well;
But let me not, my friend, your envy raise,
No! on my life, your patience has my praise.'

His friend, though silent, felt the scorn implied—
'What need of patience?' to himself he cried:
'Better a woman o'er her house to rule,   90
Than a poor child just hurried from her school;
Who has no care, yet never lives at ease;
Unfit to rule, and indisposed to please;
What if he govern, there his boast should end,
No husband's power can make a slave his friend.'

It was the custom of these friends to meet
With a few neighbours in a neighbouring street;
Where Counter ofttimes would occasion seize,
To move his silent friend by words like these:
'A man,' said he, 'if govern'd by his wife,   100
Gives up his rank and dignity in life;
Now better fate befalls my friend and me'—
He spoke, and look'd th' approving smile to see.

The quiet partner, when he chose to speak,
Desired his friend, 'another theme to seek;
When thus they met, he judged that state-affairs
And such important subjects should be theirs:'
But still the partner, in his lighter vein,
Would cause in Clubb affliction or disdain;
It made him anxious to detect the cause   110
Of all that boasting—'Wants my friend applause?
This plainly proves him not at perfect ease,
For, felt he pleasure, he would wish to please.—
These triumphs here for some regrets atone—
Men who are blest let other men alone.'
Thus made suspicious, he observed and saw
His friend each night at early hour withdraw;

He sometimes mention'd Juliet's tender nerves,
And what attention such a wife deserves:
'In this,' thought Clubb, 'full sure some mystery lies—   120
He laughs at me, yet he with much complies,
And all his vaunts of bliss are proud apologies.'

With such ideas treasured in his breast,
He grew composed, and let his anger rest,
Till Counter once (when wine so long went round
That friendship and discretion both were drown'd)
Began in teasing and triumphant mood
His evening banter—'Of all earthly good,
The best,' he said, 'was an obedient spouse,
Such as my friend's—that every one allows: 130
What if she wishes his designs to know?
It is because she would her praise bestow;
What if she wills that he remain at home?
She knows that mischief may from travel come.
I, who am free to venture where I please,
Have no such kind preventing checks as these;
But mine is double duty, first to guide
Myself aright, then rule a house beside;
While this our friend, more happy than the free,
Resigns all power, and laughs at liberty.'   140

'By Heaven,' said Clubb, 'excuse me if I swear,
I'll bet a hundred guineas, if he dare,
That uncontroll'd I will such freedoms take,
That he will fear to equal—there's my stake.'

'A match!' said Counter, much by wine inflamed;
'But we are friends—let smaller stake be named:
Wine for our future meeting, that will I
Take and no more—what perils shall we try?'
'Let's to Newmarket,' Clubb replied; 'or choose
Yourself the place, and what you like to lose;   150
And he who first returns, or fears to go,
Forfeits his cash—' Said Counter, 'Be it so.'

The friends around them saw with much delight
The social war, and hail'd the pleasant night;
Nor would they further hear the cause discuss'd,
Afraid the recreant heart of Clubb to trust.

Now sober thoughts return'd as each withdrew,
And of the subject took a serious view;
''Twas wrong,' thought Counter, 'and will grieve my
    love;'
''Twas wrong,' thought Clubb, 'my wife will not
    approve; 160
But friends were present; I must try the thing,
Or with my folly half the town will ring.'

He sought his lady—'Madam, I'm to blame,
But was reproach'd, and could not bear the shame;
Here in my folly—for 'tis best to say
The very truth—I've sworn to have my way;
To that Newmarket—(though I hate the place,
And have no taste or talents for a race,
Yet so it is—well, now prepare to chide—)
I laid a wager that I dared to ride; 170
And I must go: by Heaven, if you resist
I shall be scorn'd, and ridiculed, and hiss'd;
Let me with grace before my friends appear,
You know the truth, and must not be severe;
He too must go, but that he will of course;
Do you consent?—I never think of force.'

'You never need,' the worthy dame replied;
'The husband's honour is the woman's pride;
If I in trifles be the wilful wife,
Still for your credit I would lose my life; 180
Go! and when fix'd the day of your return,
Stay longer yet, and let the blockheads learn,
That though a wife may sometimes wish to rule,
She would not make th' indulgent man a fool;
I would at times advise—but idle they
Who think th' assenting husband *must* obey.'

The happy man, who thought his lady right
In other cases, was assured to-night;
Then for the day with proud delight prepared,
To show his doubting friends how much he dared.   190

Counter—who grieving sought his bed, his rest
Broken by pictures of his love distress'd—
With soft and winning speech the fair prepared;
'She all his councils, comforts, pleasures shared:
She was assured he loved her from his soul,
She never knew and need not fear control;
But so it happen'd—he was grieved at heart,.
It happen'd so, that they awhile must part—
A little time—the distance was but short,
And business call'd him—he despised the sport;   200
But to Newmarket he engaged to ride,
With his friend Clubb,' and there he stopp'd and sigh'd.

Awhile the tender creature look'd dismay'd,
Then floods of tears the call of grief obey'd:—

'She an objection! No!' she sobb'd, 'not one;
Her work was finish'd, and her race was run;
For die she must, indeed she would not live
A week alone, for all the world could give;
He too must die in that same wicked place;
It always happen'd—was a common case;   210
Among those horrid horses, jockeys, crowds,
'Twas certain death—they might bespeak their shrouds;
He would attempt a race, be sure to fall—
And she expire with terror—that was all;
With love like hers she was indeed unfit
To bear such horrors, but she must submit.'

'But for three days, my love! three days at most—'
'Enough for me; I then shall be a ghost—'
'My honour's pledged!'—'Oh! yes, my dearest life,
I know your honour must outweigh your wife;   220
But ere this absence, have you sought a friend?

I shall be dead—on whom can you depend?—
Let me one favour of your kindness crave,
Grant me the stone I mention'd for my grave.—'

'Nay, love, attend—why, bless my soul—I say
I will return—there—weep no longer—nay!—'
'Well! I obey, and to the last am true,
But spirits fail me! I must die; adieu!'

'What, madam! must?—'tis wrong—I'm angry—
    zounds!
Can I remain and lose a thousand pounds?'   230

'Go then, my love! it is a monstrous sum,
Worth twenty wives—go, love! and I am dumb—
Nor be displeased—had I the power to live,
You might be angry, now you must forgive;
Alas! I faint—ah! cruel—there's no need
Of wounds or fevers—this has done the deed.'

The lady fainted, and the husband sent
For every aid, for every comfort went;
Strong terror seized him; 'Oh! she loved so well,
And who th' effect of tenderness could tell?'   240

She now recover'd, and again began
With accent querulous—'Ah! cruel man—'
Till the sad husband, conscience-struck, confess'd,
'Twas very wicked with his friend to jest;
For now he saw that those who were obey'd,
Could like the most subservient feel afraid;
And though a wife might not dispute the will
Of her liege lord, she could prevent it still.

The morning came, and Clubb prepared to ride
With a smart boy, his servant and his guide;   250
When, ere he mounted on the ready steed,
Arrived a letter, and he stopp'd to read.

'My friend,' he read—'our journey I decline,
A heart too tender for such strife is mine;
Yours is the triumph, be you so inclined;
But you are too considerate and kind:
In tender pity to my Juliet's fears
I thus relent, o'ercome by love and tears;
She knows your kindness; I have heard her say,
A man like you 'tis pleasure to obey: 260
Each faithful wife, like ours, must disapprove
Such dangerous trifling with connubial love;
What has the idle world, my friend, to do
With our affairs? they envy me and you:
What if I could my gentle spouse command—
Is that a cause I should her tears withstand?
And what if you, a friend of peace, submit
To one you love—is that a theme for wit?
'Twas wrong, and I shall henceforth judge it weak
Both of submission and control to speak: 270
Be it agreed that all contention cease,
And no such follies vex our future peace;
Let each keep guard against domestic strife,
And find nor slave nor tyrant in his wife.'

'Agreed,' said Clubb, 'with all my soul agreed'—
And to the boy, delighted, gave his steed;
'I think my friend has well his mind express'd,
And I assent; such things are not a jest.'

'True,' said the wife, 'no longer he can hide
The truth that pains him by his wounded pride: 280
Your friend has found it not an easy thing,
Beneath his yoke, this yielding soul to bring;
These weeping willows, though they seem inclined
By every breeze, yet not the strongest wind
Can from their bent divert this weak but stubborn kind;
Drooping they seek your pity to excite,
But 'tis at once their nature and delight;
Such women feel not; while they sigh and weep,

'Tis but their habit—their affections sleep;
They are like ice that in the hand we hold,⁣⁣   290
So very melting, yet so very cold;
On such affection let no man rely,
The husbands suffer, and the ladies sigh:
But your friend's offer, let us kindly take,
And spare his pride for his vexation's sake;
For he has found, and through his life will find,
'Tis easiest dealing with the firmest mind—
More just when it resists, and, when it yields, more kind.'

From *Posthumous Tales* (1834)

SILFORD HALL; or, THE HAPPY DAY

WITHIN a village, many a mile from town,
A place of small resort and no renown;—
Save that it form'd a way, and gave a name
To SILFORD HALL, it made no claim to fame;—
It was the gain of some, the pride of all,
That travellers stopt to ask for SILFORD HALL.
 Small as it was, the place could boast a School,
In which *Nathaniel Perkin* bore the rule.
Not mark'd for learning deep, or talents rare,
But for his varying tasks and ceaseless care;⁣⁣   10
Some forty boys, the sons of thrifty men,
He taught to read, and part to use the pen;
While, by more studious care, a favourite few
Increased his pride—for if the Scholar knew
Enough for praise, say what the Teacher's due?—
These to his presence, slates in hand, moved on,
And a grim smile their feats in figures won.
 This Man of Letters woo'd in early life
The Vicar's maiden, whom he made his wife.
She too can read, as by her song she proves—⁣⁣   20
The song Nathaniel made about their loves:
Five rosy girls, and one fair boy, increased
The Father's care, whose labours seldom ceased.

No day of rest was his. If now, and then,
His boys for play laid by the book and pen,
For Lawyer Slow there was some deed to write,
Or some young farmer's letter to indite,
Or land to measure, or, with legal skill,
To frame some yeoman's widow's peevish will;
And on the Sabbath,—when his neighbours drest,   30
To hear their duties, and to take their rest—
Then, when the Vicar's periods ceased to flow,
Was heard Nathaniel, in his seat below.

Such were his labours; but the time is come
When his son *Peter* clears the hours of gloom,
And brings him aid: though yet a boy, he shares
In staid Nathaniel's multifarious cares.
A king his father, he, a prince, has rule—
The first of subjects, viceroy of the school:
But though a prince within that realm he reigns,   40
Hard is the part his duteous soul sustains.
He with his Father, o'er the furrow'd land,
Draws the long chain in his uneasy hand,
And neatly forms at home, what there they rudely plann'd.
Content, for all his labour, if he gains
Some words of praise, and sixpence for his pains.
Thus many a hungry day the Boy has fared,
And would have ask'd a dinner, had he dared.
When boys are playing, he, for hours of school
Has sums to set, and copy-books to rule;   50
When all are met, for some sad dunce afraid,
He, by allowance, lends his timely aid—
Taught at the student's failings to connive,
Yet keep his Father's dignity alive:
For ev'n Nathaniel fears, and might offend,
If too severe, the farmer, now his friend;
Or her, that farmer's lady, who well knows
Her boy is bright, and needs nor threats nor blows.
This seem'd to Peter hard; and he was loth,
T' obey and rule, and have the·cares of both—   60
To miss the master's dignity, and yet,

No portion of the school-boy's play to get.
To him the Fiend, as once to Launcelot, cried,
'Run from thy wrongs!'—'Run where?' his fear replied:
'Run!'—said the Tempter, 'if but hard thy fare,
Hard is it now—it *may* be mended there.'
  But still, though tempted, he refused to part,
And felt the Mother clinging at his heart.
Nor this alone—he, in that weight of care,
Had help, and bore it as a man should bear.   70
A drop of comfort in his cup was thrown;
It was his treasure, and it was his own.
His Father's shelves contained a motley store
Of letter'd wealth; and this he might explore.
A part his mother in her youth had gain'd,
A part Nathaniel from his club obtain'd,
And part—a well-worn kind—from sire to son remain'd.
  He sought his Mother's hoard, and there he found
Romance in sheets, and poetry unbound;
Soft Tales of Love, which never damsel read,   80
But tears of pity stain'd her virgin bed.
There were Jane Shore and Rosamond the Fair,
And humbler heroines frail as these were there;
There was a tale of one forsaken Maid,
Who till her death the work of vengeance stay'd;
Her Lover, then at sea, while round him stood
A dauntless crew, the angry ghost pursued;
In a small boat, without an oar or sail,
She came to call him, nor would force avail,
Nor prayer; but, conscience-stricken, down he leapt,   90
And o'er his corse the closing billows slept;
All vanish'd then! but of the crew were some,
Wondering whose ghost would on the morrow come.
  A learned Book was there, and in it schemes
How to cast Fortunes and interpret Dreams;
Ballads were there of Lover's bliss or bale,
The Kitchen Story, and the Nursery Tale.
His hungry mind disdain'd not humble food,
And read with relish keen of Robin Hood;

Of him, all-powerful made by magic gift,   100
And Giants slain—of mighty Hickerthrift;
Through Crusoe's Isle delighted had he stray'd,
Nocturnal visits had to witches paid,
Gliding through haunted scenes, enraptured and afraid.

A loftier shelf with real books was graced,
Bound, or part bound, and ranged in comely taste;
Books of high mark, the mind's more solid food,
Which some might think the owner understood;
But Fluxions, Sections, Algebraic lore,
Our Peter left for others to explore,   110
And quickly turning to a favourite kind,
Found, what rejoiced him at his heart to find.

Sir Walter wrote not then, or He by whom
Such gain and glory to Sir Walter come—
That Fairy-Helper, by whose secret aid,
Such views of life are to the world convey'd—
As inspiration known in after-times,
The sole assistant in his prose or rhymes.
But there were fictions wild that please the boy,
Which men, too, read, condemn, reject, enjoy—   120
Arabian Nights. and Persian Tales were there,
One volume each, and both the worse for wear;
There by Quarles' Emblems, Esop's Fables stood,
The coats in tatters, and the cuts in wood.
There, too, 'The English History,' by the pen
Of Doctor Cooke, and other learned men,
In numbers, sixpence each; by these was seen,
And highly prized, the Monthly Magazine;—
Not such as now will men of taste engage,
But the cold gleanings of a former age,   130
Scraps cut from sermons, scenes removed from plays,
With heads of heroes famed in Tyburn's palmy days.

The rest we pass—though Peter pass'd them not,
But here his cares and labours all forgot:
Stain'd, torn, and blotted every noble page,
Stood the chief poets of a former age—
And of the present; not their works complete,

But in such portions as on bulks we meet,
The refuse of the shops, thrown down upon the street.
There Shakspeare, Spenser, Milton found a place,   140
With some a nameless, some a shameless race,
Which many a weary walker resting reads,
And, pondering o'er the short relief, proceeds,
While others lingering pay the written sum,
Half loth, but longing for delight to come.
    Of the Youth's morals we would something speak;
Taught by his Mother what to shun or seek:
She show'd the heavenly way, and in his youth,
Press'd on his yielding mind the Gospel truth,
How weak is man, how much to ill inclined,   150
And where his help is placed, and how to find.
These words of weight sank deeply in his breast,
And awful Fear and holy Hope imprest.
He shrank from vice, and at the startling view,
As from an adder in his path, withdrew.
All else was cheerful. Peter's easy mind
To the gay scenes of village-life inclined.
The lark that soaring sings his notes of joy,
Was not more lively than th' awaken'd boy.
Yet oft with this a softening sadness dwelt,   160
While, feeling thus, he marvell'd why he felt.
'I am not sorry,' said the Boy, 'but still,
The tear will drop—I wonder why it will!'
    His books, his walks, his musing, morn and eve,
Gave such impressions as such minds receive;
And with his moral and religious views
Wove the wild fancies of an Infant-Muse,
Inspiring thoughts that he could not express,
Obscure sublime! his secret happiness.
Oft would he strive for words, and oft begin   170
To frame in verse the views he had within;
But ever fail'd: for how can words explain
The unform'd ideas of a teeming brain?
    Such was my Hero, whom I would portray
In one exploit—the Hero of a Day.

At six miles' distance from his native town
Stood Silford Hall, a seat of much renown—
Computed miles, such weary travellers ride,
When they in chance wayfaring men confide.
Beauty and grandeur were within; around,   180
Lawn, wood, and water; the delicious ground
Had parks where deer disport, had fields where game
    abound.
Fruits of all tastes in spacious gardens grew;
And flowers of every scent and every hue,
That native in more favour'd climes arise,
Are here protected from th' inclement skies.
    To this fair place, with mingled pride and shame
This lad of learning without knowledge came—
Shame for his conscious ignorance—and pride
To this fair seat in this gay style to ride.   190
    The cause that brought him was a small account,
His father's due, and he must take the amount,
And sign a stamp'd receipt! this done, he might
Look all around him, and enjoy the sight.
    So far to walk was, in his mother's view,
More than her darling Peter ought to do;
Peter indeed knew more, but he would hide
His better knowledge, for he wish'd to ride;
So had his father's nag, a beast so small,
That if he fell, he had not far to fall.   200
    His fond and anxious mother in his best,
Her darling child for the occasion drest:
All in his coat of green she clothed her boy,
And stood admiring with a mother's joy:
Large was it made and long, as meant to do
For Sunday-service, when he older grew—
Not brought in daily use in one year's wear or two.
White was his waistcoat, and what else he wore
Had clothed the lamb or parent ewe before.
In all the mother show'd her care or skill;   210
A riband black she tied beneath his frill;
Gave him his stockings, white as driven snow,

And bad him heed the miry way below;
On the black varnish of the comely shoe,
Shone the large buckle of a silvery hue.
Boots he had worn, had he such things possest—
But bootless grief!—he was full proudly drest;
Full proudly look'd, and light he was of heart,
When thus for Silford Hall prepared to start.

Nathaniel's self with joy the stripling eyed,   220
And gave a shilling with a father's pride;
Rules of politeness too with pomp he gave,
And show'd the lad how scholars should behave.

Ere yet he left her home, the Mother told—
For she had seen—what things he should behold.
There, she related, her young eyes had view'd
Stone figures shaped like naked flesh and blood,
Which, in the hall and up the gallery placed,
Were proofs, they told her, of a noble taste;
Nor she denied—but, in a public hall,   230
Her judgment taken, she had clothed them all.
There, too, were station'd, each upon its seat,
Half forms of men, without their hands and feet;
These and what more within that hall might be
She saw, and oh! how long'd her son to see!
Yet could he hope to view that noble place,
Who dared not look the porter in the face?

Forth went the pony, and the rider's knees
Cleaved to her sides—he did not ride with ease;
One hand a whip, and one a bridle held,   240
In case the pony falter'd or rebell'd.

The village boys beheld him as he pass'd,
And looks of envy on the hero cast;
But he was meek, nor let his pride appear,
Nay, truth to speak, he felt a sense of fear,
Lest the rude beast, unmindful of the rein,
Should take a fancy to turn back again.

He found, and wonder 'tis he found, his way,
The orders many that he must obey:
'Now to the right, then left, and now again   250

Directly onward, through the winding lane;
Then, half way o'er the common, by the mill,
Turn from the cottage and ascend the hill,
Then—spare the pony, boy!—as you ascend—
You see the Hall, and that's your journey's end.'
　　Yes, he succeeded, not remembering aught
Of this advice, but by his pony taught.
Soon as he doubted he the bridle threw
On the steed's neck, and said—'Remember you!'
For oft the creature had his father borne,　　　　260
Sound on his way, and safe on his return.
So he succeeded, and the modest youth
Gave praise, where praise had been assign'd by truth.
　　His business done,—for fortune led his way
To him whose office was such debts to pay,
The farmer-bailiff, but he saw no more
Than a small room, with bare and oaken floor,
A desk with books thereon—he'd seen such things before;
'Good day!' he said, but lingered as he spoke
'Good day,' and gazed about with serious look;　　270
Then slowly moved, and then delay'd awhile,
In dumb dismay which raised a lordly smile
In those who eyed him—then again moved on,
As all might see, unwilling to be gone.
　　While puzzled thus, and puzzling all about,
Involved, absorb'd, in some bewildering doubt,
A lady enter'd, Madam Johnson call'd,
Within whose presence stood the lad appall'd.
A learned Lady this, who knew the names
Of all the pictures in the golden frames;　　　　280
Could every subject, every painter, tell,
And on their merits and their failures dwell;
And if perchance there was a slight mistake—
These the most known on such matters make.
　　'And what dost mean, my pretty lad?' she cried,
'Dost stay or go?'—He first for courage tried,
Then for fit words,—then boldly he replied,
That he 'would give a hundred pounds, if so

He had them, all about that house to go;
For he had heard that it contain'd such things   290
As never house could boast, except the king's.'
  The ruling Lady, smiling, said, 'In truth
Thou shalt behold them all, my pretty youth.
Tom! first the creature to the stable lead,
Let it be fed; and you, my child, must feed;
For three good hours must pass e'er dinner come,'—
'Supper,' thought he, 'she means, our time at home.'
  First was he feasted to his heart's content,
Then, all in rapture, with the Lady went;
Through rooms immense, and galleries wide and tall,   300
He walk'd entranced—he breathed in Silford Hall.
  Now could he look on that delightful place,
The glorious dwelling of a princely race;
His vast delight was mixed with equal awe,
There was such magic in the things he saw.
Oft standing still, with open mouth and eyes,
Turn'd here and there, alarm'd as one who tries
T' escape from something strange, that would before
    him rise.
The wall would part, and beings without name
Would come—for such to his adventures came.   310
Hence undefined and solemn terror press'd
Upon his mind, and all his powers possess'd.
All he had read of magic, every charm,
Were he alone, might come and do him harm:
But his gaze rested on his friendly guide—
'I'm safe,' he thought, 'so long as you abide.'
  In one large room was found a bed of state—
'And can they soundly sleep beneath such weight,
Where they may figures in the night explore,
Form'd by the dim light dancing on the floor   320
From the far window; mirrors broad and high
Doubling each terror to the anxious eye?—
'Tis strange,' thought Peter, 'that such things produce
No fear in *her*; but there is much in use.'
  On that reflecting brightness, passing by,

The Boy one instant fix'd his restless eye—
And saw himself: he had before descried
His face in one his mother's store supplied;
But here he could his whole dimensions view,
From the pale forehead to the jet-black shoe.   330
Passing he look'd, and looking, grieved to pass
From the fair figure smiling in the glass.
'Twas so Narcissus saw the boy advance
In the dear fount, and met th' admiring glance
So loved—But no! our happier boy admired,
Not the slim form, but what the form attired,—
The riband, shirt, and frill, all pure and clean,
The white ribb'd stockings, and the coat of green.

    The Lady now appear'd to move away—
And this was threat'ning; for he dared not stay,   340
Lost and alone; but earnestly he pray'd—
'Oh! do not leave me—I am not afraid,
But 'tis so lonesome; I shall never find
My way alone, no better than the blind.'

    The Matron kindly to the Boy replied,
'Trust in my promise, I will be thy guide.'
Then to the Chapel moved the friendly pair,
And well for Peter that his guide was there!
Dim, silent, solemn was the scene—he felt
The cedar's power, that so unearthly smelt;   350
And then the stain'd, dark, narrow windows threw
Strange, partial beams on pulpit, desk, and pew:
Upon the altar, glorious to behold,
Stood a vast pair of candlesticks in gold!
With candles tall, and large, and firm, and white,
Such as the halls of giant-kings would light.
There was an organ, too, but now unseen;
A long black curtain served it for a screen;
Not so the clock, that both by night and day,
Click'd the short moments as they pass'd away.   360

    'Is this a church? and does the parson read'—
Said Peter—'here?—I mean a church indeed.'—
'Indeed it is, or as a church is used,'

Was the reply,—and Peter deeply mused,
Not without awe. His sadness to dispel,
They sought the gallery, and then all was well.
 Yet enter'd there, although so clear his mind
From every fear substantial and defined,
Yet there remain'd some touch of native fear—
Of something awful to the eye and ear—   370
A ghostly voice might sound—a ghost itself appear.
 There noble Pictures fill'd his mind with joy—
He gazed and thought, and was no more the boy;
And Madam heard him speak, with some surprise,
Of heroes known to him from histories.
He knew the actors in the deeds of old,—
He could the Roman marvels all unfold.
He to his guide a theme for wonder grew,
At once so little and so much he knew—
Little of what was passing every day,   380
And much of that which long had pass'd away;—
So like a man, and yet so like a child,
That his good friend stood wond'ring as she smiled.
 The Scripture Pieces caused a serious awe,
And he with reverence look'd on all he saw;
His pious wonder he express'd aloud,
And at the Saviour Form devoutly bow'd.
 Portraits he pass'd, admiring; but with pain
Turn'd from some objects, nor would look again.
He seem'd to think that something wrong was done,   390
When crimes were shown he blush'd to look upon.
Not so his guide—'What youth is that?' she cried,
'That handsome stripling at the lady's side;
Can you inform me how the youth is named?'
He answered, '*Joseph*;' but he look'd ashamed.
'Well, and what then? Had you been Joseph, boy!
Would you have been so peevish and so coy?'
Our hero answer'd, with a glowing face,
'His mother told him he should pray for grace.'
A transient cloud o'ercast the matron's brow;   400
She seem'd disposed to laugh—but knew not how;

147

Silent awhile, then placid she appear'd—
"'Tis but a child,' she thought, and all was clear'd.
  No—laugh she could not; still, the more she sought
To hide her thoughts, the more of his she caught.
A hundred times she had these pictures named,
And never felt perplex'd, disturb'd, asham'd;
Yet now the feelings of a lad so young
Call'd home her thoughts and paralysed her tongue.
She pass'd the offensive pictures silent by,   410
With one reflecting, self-reproving sigh;
Reasoning how habit will the mind entice
To approach and gaze upon the bounds of vice,
As men, by custom, from some cliff's vast height,
Look pleased, and make their danger their delight.
  'Come, let us on!—see there a Flemish view,
A Country Fair, and all as Nature true.
See there the merry creatures, great and small,
Engaged in drinking, gaming, dancing all,
Fiddling or fighting—all in drunken joy!'—   420
'But is this Nature?' said the wondering Boy.
  'Be sure it is! and those Banditti there—
Observe the faces, forms, the eyes, the air:
See rage, revenge, remorse, disdain, despair!'
  'And is that Nature, too?' the stripling cried.—
'Corrupted Nature,' said the serious guide.
  She then display'd her knowledge.—'That, my dear,
Is call'd a Titian, this a Guido here,
And yon a Claude—you see that lovely light,
So soft and solemn, neither day nor night.'   430
  'Yes!' quoth the Boy, 'and there is just the breeze,
That curls the water, and that fans the trees;
The ships that anchor in that pleasant bay
All look so safe and quiet—Claude, you say?'
  On a small picture Peter gazed and stood
In admiration—"twas so dearly good.'
'For how much money think you, then, my Lad,
Is such a "dear good picture" to be had?
'Tis a famed master's work—a Gerard Dow,

At least the seller told the buyer so.'   440
   'I tell the price!' quoth Peter—'I as soon
Could tell the price of pictures in the moon;
But I have heard, when the great race was done,
How much was offer'd for the horse that won.'—
   'A thousand pounds: but, look the country round,
And, may be, ten such horses might be found;
While, ride or run where'er you choose to go,
You'll nowhere find so fine a Gerard Dow.'
   'If this be true,' says Peter, 'then, of course,
You'd rate the picture higher than the horse.'   450
   'Why, thou'rt a reasoner, Boy!' the lady cried;
'But see that Infant on the other side;
'Tis by Sir Joshua. Did you ever see
A Babe so charming?'—'No, indeed,' said he;
'I wonder how he could that look invent,
That seems so sly, and yet so innocent.'
   In this long room were various Statues seen,
And Peter gazed thereon with awe-struck mien.
   'Why look so earnest, Boy?'—'Because they bring
To me a story of an awful thing.'—   460
'Tell then thy story.'——He who never stay'd
For words or matter, instantly obey'd.—
   'A holy pilgrim to a city sail'd,
Where every sin o'er sinful men prevail'd;
Who, when he landed, look'd in every street,
As he was wont, a busy crowd to meet;
But now of living beings found he none,
Death had been there, and turn'd them all to stone;
All in an instant, as they were employ'd,
Was life in every living man destroy'd—   470
The rich, the poor, the timid, and the bold,
Made in a moment such as we behold.'
   'Come, my good lad, you've yet a room to see.
Are you awake?'—'I am amazed,' said he;
'I know they're figures form'd by human skill,
But 'tis so awful, and this place so still!
   'And what is this?' said Peter, who had seen

A long wide table, with its cloth of green,
Its net-work pockets, and its studs of gold—
For such they seem'd, and precious to behold.   480
There too were ivory balls, and one was red,
Laid with long sticks upon the soft green bed,
And printed tables, on the wall beside—
'Oh! what are these?' the wondering Peter cried.

'This, my good lad, is call'd the Billiard-room,'
Answer'd his guide, 'and here the gentry come,
And with these maces and these cues they play,
At their spare time, or in a rainy day.'

'And what this chequer'd box?—for play, I guess?'—
'You judge it right; 'tis for the game of Chess.   490
There! take your time, examine what you will,
There's King, Queen, Knight,—it is a game of skill:
And these are Bishops; you the difference see.'—
'What! do they make a game of *them*?' quoth he.—
'Bishops, like Kings,' she said, 'are here but names;
Not that I answer for their Honours' games.'

All round the house did Peter go, and found
Food for his wonder all the house around.
There guns of various bore, and rods, and lines,
And all that man for deed of death designs,   500
In beast, or bird, or fish, or worm, or fly—
Life in these last must means of death supply;
The living bait is gorged, and both the victims die.
'God gives man leave his creatures to destroy.'—
'What! for his sport?' replied the pitying Boy.—
'Nay,' said the Lady, 'why the sport condemn?
As die they must, 'tis much the same to them.'
Peter had doubts; but with so kind a friend,
He would not on a dubious point contend.

Much had he seen, and every thing he saw   510
Excited pleasure not unmix'd with awe.
Leaving each room, he turn'd as if once more
To enjoy the pleasure that he felt before—
What then must their possessors feel! how grand
And happy they who can such joys command!

For they may pleasures all their lives pursue,
The winter pleasures, and the summer's too—
Pleasures for every hour in every day—
Oh! how their time must pass in joy away!'
    So Peter said.—Replied the courteous Dame: 520
'What you call pleasure scarcely owns the name.
The very changes of amusement prove
There's nothing that deserves a lasting love.
They hunt, they course, they shoot, they fish, they game;
The objects vary, though the end the same—
A search for that which flies them; no, my Boy!
'Tis not enjoyment, 'tis pursuit of joy.'
    Peter was thoughtful—thinking, What! not these,
Who can command, or purchase, what they please—
Whom many serve, who only speak the word,   530
And they have all that earth or seas afford—
All that can charm the mind and please the eye—
And *they* not happy!—but I'll ask her why.
    So Peter ask'd.—"'Tis not,' she said, 'for us,
Their Honours' inward feelings to discuss;
But if they're happy, they would still confess
'Tis not these things that make their happiness.
    'Look from this window! at his work behold
Yon gardener's helper—he is poor and old,
He not one thing of all you see can call   540
His own; but, haply, he o'erlooks them all.
Hear him! he whistles through his work, or stops
But to admire his labours and his crops:
To-day as every former day he fares,
And for the morrow has nor doubts nor cares;
Pious and cheerful, proud when he can please,
Judge if Joe Tompkin want such things as these.
    'Come, let us forward!' and she walk'd in haste
To a large room, itself a work of taste,
But chiefly valued for the works that drew   550
The eyes of Peter—this indeed was new,
Was most imposing—Books of every kind
Were there disposed, the food for every mind.

With joy perplex'd, round cast he wondering eyes,
Still in his joy, and dumb in his surprise.
　　Above, beneath, around, on every side,
Of every form and size were Books descried;
Like Bishop Hatto, when the rats drew near,
And war's new dangers waked his guilty fear,
When thousands came beside, behind, before,　　**560**
And up and down came on ten thousand more;
A tail'd and whisker'd army, each with claws
As sharp as needles, and with teeth like saws,—
So fill'd with awe, and wonder in his looks,
Stood Peter, 'midst this multitude of Books;
But guiltless he and fearless; yet he sigh'd
To think what treasures were to him denied.
　　But wonder ceases on continued view;
And the Boy sharp for close inspection grew.
Prints on the table he at first survey'd,　　**570**
Then to the Books his full attention paid.
At first, from tome to tome, as fancy led,
He view'd the binding, and the titles read;
Lost in delight, and with his freedom pleased,
Then three huge folios from their shelf he seized;
Fixing on one, with prints of every race,
Of beast and bird most rare in every place,—
Serpents, the giants of their tribe, whose prey
Are giants too—a wild ox once a day;
Here the fierce tiger, and the desert's kings,　　**580**
And all that move on feet, or fins, or wings—
Most rare and strange; a second volume told
Of battles dire, and dreadful to behold,
On sea or land, and fleets dispersed in storms;
A third has all creative fancy forms,—
Hydra and dire chimera, deserts rude,
And ruins grand, enriching solitude:
Whatever was, or was supposed to be,
Saw Peter here, and still desired to see.
　　Again he look'd, but happier had he been,　　**590**
That Book of Wonders he had never seen;

For there were tales of men of wicked mind,
And how the Foe of Man deludes mankind.
Magic and murder every leaf bespread—
Enchanted halls, and chambers of the dead,
And ghosts that haunt the scenes where once the victims
    bled.
  Just at this time, when Peter's heart began
To admit the fear that shames the valiant man,
He paused—but why? 'Here's one my guard to be;
When thus protected, none can trouble me:'—   600
Then rising look'd he round, and lo! alone was he.
  Three ponderous doors, with locks of shining brass,
Seem'd to invite the trembling Boy to pass;
But fear forbad, till fear itself supplied
The place of courage, and at length he tried.
He grasp'd the key—Alas! though great his need,
The key turn'd not, the bolt would not recede.
Try then again; for what will not distress?
Again he tried, and with the same success.
Yet one remains, remains untried one door—   610
A failing hope, for two had fail'd before;
But a bold prince, with fifty doors in sight,
Tried forty-nine before he found the right;
Before he mounted on the brazen horse,
And o'er the walls pursued his airy course.
So his cold hand on this last key he laid:
'Now turn,' said he; the treacherous bolt obey'd—
The door receded—bringing full in view
The dim, dull chapel, pulpit, desk, and pew.
  It was not right—it would have vex'd a saint;   620
And Peter's anger rose above restraint.
'Was this her love,' he cried, 'to bring me here,
Among the dead, to die myself with fear!'—
For Peter judged, with monuments around,
The dead must surely in the place be found:—
'With cold to shiver, and with hunger pine—
"We'll see the rooms," she said, "before we dine;"
And spake so kind! That window gives no light:

Here is enough the boldest man to fright;
It hardly now is day, and soon it will be night.' 630
    Deeply he sigh'd, nor from his heart could chase
The dread of dying in that dismal place;
Anger and sorrow in his bosom strove,
And banish'd all that yet remain'd of love;
When soon despair had seized the trembling Boy,
But hark, a voice! the sound of peace and joy.
    'Where art thou, lad?'—'Oh! here am I, in doubt,
And sorely frighten'd—can you let me out?'
'Oh! yes, my child; it was indeed a sin,
Forgetful as I was, to bolt you in. 640
I left you reading, and from habit lock'd
The door behind me, but in truth am shock'd
To serve you thus; but we will make amends
For such mistake. Come, cheerly, we are friends.'
    'Oh! yes,' said Peter, quite alive to be
So kindly used, and have so much to see,
And having so much seen; his way he spied,
Forgot his peril, and rejoin'd his guide.
    Now all beheld, his admiration raised,
The lady thank'd, her condescension praised, 650
And fix'd the hour for dinner, forth the Boy
Went in a tumult of o'erpowering joy,
To view the gardens, and what more was found
In the wide circuit of that spacious ground,
Till, with his thoughts bewilder'd, and oppress'd
With too much feeling, he inclined to rest.
    Then in the park he sought its deepest shade,
By trees more aged than the mansion made,
That ages stood; and there unseen a brook
Ran not unheard, and thus our traveller spoke,— 660
'I am so happy, and have such delight,
I cannot bear to see another sight;
It wearies one like work;' and so, with deep
Unconscious sigh—he laid him down to sleep.
    Thus he reclining slept, and, oh! the joy
That in his dreams possess'd the happy boy,—

Composed of all he knew, and all he read,
Heard, or conceived, the living and the dead.
　The Caliph Haroun, walking forth by night
To see young David and Goliath fight,　　　　　　　670
Rose on his passive fancy—then appear'd
The fleshless forms of beings scorn'd or fear'd
By just or evil men—the baneful race
Of spirits restless, borne from place to place:
Rivers of blood from conquer'd armies ran,
The flying steed was by, the marble man;
Then danced the fairies round their pygmy queen,
And their feet twinkled on the dewy green,
All in the moon-beams' glory. As they fled,
The mountain loadstone rear'd its fatal head,　　680
And drew the iron-bolted ships on shore,
Where he distinctly heard the billows roar,—
Mix'd with a living voice of—'Youngster, sleep no more,
But haste to dinner.' Starting from the ground,
The waking boy obey'd that welcome sound.
　He went and sat, with equal shame and pride,
A welcome guest at Madam Johnson's side.
At his right hand was Mistress Kitty placed,
And Lucy, maiden sly, the stripling faced.
Then each the proper seat at table took—　　　　690
Groom, butler, footman, laundress, coachman, cook;
For all their station and their office knew,
Nor sat as rustics or the rabble do.
　The Youth to each the due attention paid,
And hob-or-nob'd with Lady Charlotte's maid;
With much respect each other they address'd,
And all encouraged their enchanted guest.
Wine, fruit, and sweetmeats closed repast so long,
And Mistress Flora sang an opera song.
　Such was the Day the happy Boy had spent,　　700
And forth delighted from the Hall he went:
Bowing his thanks, he mounted on his steed,
More largely fed than he was wont to feed;
And well for Peter that his pony knew

From whence he came, the road he should pursue;
For the young rider had his mind estranged
From all around, disturb'd and disarranged,
In pleasing tumult, in a dream of bliss,
Enjoy'd but seldom in a world like this.

But though the pleasures of the Day were past,— 710
For lively pleasures are not form'd to last,—
And though less vivid they became, less strong,
Through life they lived, and were enjoy'd as long.
So deep the impression of that happy Day,
Not time nor cares could wear it all away;
Ev'n to the last, in his declining years,
He told of all his glories, all his fears.

How blithely forward in that morn he went,
How blest the hours in that fair palace spent,
How vast that Mansion, sure for monarch plann'd, 720
The rooms so many, and yet each so grand,—
Millions of books in one large hall were found,
And glorious pictures every room around;
Beside that strangest of the wonders there,
That house itself contain'd a house of prayer.

He told of park and wood, of sun and shade,
And how the lake below the lawn was made:
He spake of feasting such as never boy,
Taught in his school, was fated to enjoy—
Of ladies' maids as ladies' selves who dress'd, 730
And her, his friend, distinguish'd from the rest,
By grandeur in her look, and state that she possess'd.
He pass'd not one; his grateful mind o'erflow'd
With sense of all he felt, and they bestow'd.

He spake of every office, great or small,
Within, without, and spake with praise of all—
So pass'd the happy Boy, that Day at Silford Hall.

NOTES

THE PARISH REGISTER

As Crabbe explains in the first six lines of the poem, *The Parish Register* is cast in the form of the reflections of the clergyman of the parish as he looks through the entries in the parish register for a single year; the three parts being entitled respectively *Baptisms*, *Marriages* and *Burials*. Part I is here printed in full, except for the omission of the long section of general introduction, which consists chiefly of a detailed description of the cottage of an industrious peasant contrasted with the dwellings of 'the Poor when improvident and vicious'.

Page 29   PART I. BAPTISMS

l. 5.   *nymphs or swains*. These conventional poetic terms for 'young women' and 'countrymen' (used particularly during the seventeenth and eighteenth centuries for the idealised shepherds and shepherdesses of pastoral poetry) are part of the armoury of poetic diction which Crabbe continued to employ in all except his very last works.

ll. 7-14.   It had been customary to start any long poem, particularly an epic or a pastoral, with an invocation of the Muse's aid. Crabbe is here explicitly rejecting the epic and pastoral conventions, and insisting that his poem will instead be a plain realistic account of ordinary people; it is, in fact, to be based not upon poetic imagination but upon a clergyman's first-hand knowledge and observation, supplemented by the parish records.

l. 12.   *parts*. Talents, abilities.

l. 33.   The 'prize-money' derived from the sale of enemy property captured at sea was, at this period, divided among the officers and crew of the ship which made the capture, and would often amount to a considerable sum. Notice, in this connection, the Sailor's use of the word 'prize' in line 30.

l. 41.   *jean*. A strong twilled cotton fabric.

l. 49.   *churl*. In this context, the word evidently combines the sense of 'a rude, low-bred, boorish fellow' with that of 'someone who is hard and stingy in money matters'. Perhaps the phrase 'tyrant of the parish' in the next line implies someone who has shown his niggardliness while acting as parish overseer. See *The Borough*, Letter XIX, lines 230-1, and note.

l. 49.   *in bargain*. The bargaining would be over the size of the dowry which the Miller was to provide with his daughter, and possibly over the marriage-settlement to be made by the husband.

ll. 59-66.   Certain features of the rhythm and movement of these lines are particularly appropriate to the character and profession of the speaker. Can you identify and define them?

l. 71.   *the muddy cheer*. The Miller is accustomed to drink spirits (see line 25); hence this expression of contempt for the beer which he assumes is all the Sailor can afford.

l. 81.   *fond*. Cf. note on *Procrastination*, line 8.

l. 81.   *trim*. Smart, handsome.

l. 101.   *portion*. In the dual sense of (*a*) 'dowry' and (*b*) 'lot' or 'destiny'. Perhaps the sense of 'inheritance' or 'share of an estate' is also present, and the Miller is not only refusing his daughter a dowry, but also disinheriting her.

l. 106.   *higgler*. An itinerant dealer in a small way of business who bought up poultry and dairy produce, and supplied in exchange petty commodities from the shops in town.

ll. 137-8.   She is oppressed in turn by two separate evils—bodily want and misery in the present, and the fear of madness in the future.

l. 161.   *wheel*. Spinning-wheel.

l. 170.   *wrought double tides*. 'Did two days' work in one.' This idiom may have arisen out of the idea of taking advantage of both the tides in the same day, since 'tide' is sometimes used for that part of the tide during which work can be carried out in harbour.

Notice the play upon words between 'work' in the previous line, and 'wrought' (archaic past tense of the verb 'to work').

l. 174.   *their*. i.e. the wealthier farmers'.

l. 178. *nice*. Discriminating, well-judged.

ll. 181-2. In what ways is this comparison a particularly appropriate one here?

ll. 191-2. Notice here the kind of pointedness to which Crabbe's habit of playing upon words lends itself so neatly.

l. 193. *as ducks in a decoy*. A 'decoy' (still common in Crabbe's time in some parts of the countryside) was a pond out of which led narrow channels covered with network into which wild ducks could be allured and there caught.

l. 199. *churching*. The service prescribed in the Book of Common Prayer at which women after childbirth give public thanks for their safe delivery. Notice how Crabbe indicates that she is more concerned over the risk of missing this ritual than over her moral lapse.

l. 206. *quick*. Alive.

l. 213. *then*. i.e. at the wedding ceremony.

l. 232. *unportion'd*. Without a dowry.

l. 261. *hyson*. A kind of green china tea very popular in the eighteenth century, a period during which the consumption of tea by all classes had increased enormously. Though prices had come down, the customs duty on tea remained very high until towards the end of the century; and this resulted in vast quantities being smuggled in illegally from France. Parson Woodforde's casual references in his diary to 'Andrews the smuggler' make it clear that smuggling was widely accepted (and patronised) by quite respectable people.

l. 288. *Jacob's wife*. Rachel. See Genesis xxx, 1 and 2:

And when Rachel saw that she bare Jacob no children, Rachel envied her sister; and said unto Jacob, Give me children or else I die.

And Jacob's anger was kindled against Rachel: and he said, Am I in God's stead, who hath withheld from thee the fruit of the womb?

l. 289. *fond*. Foolish, unreasoning.

l. 321. *arrows number'd for the giant's hand*. See Psalm 127 in the Book of Common Prayer:

Lo, children and the fruit of the womb are an heritage and a gift that cometh of the Lord.

Like as the arrows in the hand of the giant even so are the young children.

Happy is the man that hath his quiver full of them: they shall not be ashamed when they speak with their enemies in the gate.

ll. 341-3.   Her serious looks compel her neighbours to listen to her reading the Bible aloud, instead of gossiping as they had intended.

ll. 349-411.   The botanical knowledge displayed in this passage reminds us that Crabbe was himself an expert and indefatigable student of natural history who at one time wrote an Essay on Botany in English which he laid aside 'in consequence of the remonstrances of the vice-master of Trinity College, Cambridge . . . who could not stomach the notion of degrading such a science by treating of it in a modern language'. Crabbe's satire here, however is directed not so much against this kind of 'academical peculiarity' as against the tendency to regard knowledge of botanical names as an end in itself, and in particular against the Gardener's use of high-sounding words for the sake of impressing the ignorant.

For the most part the meaning of the botanical terms can be inferred from the context. Arums and Leontodons are, in fact, the same as cuckoo-pints and dandelions. Lonicera is the botanical name for the honeysuckles, Belladonna that for deadly nightshade, and Cucumis for cucumber; while Rhus is the name of a genus of shrubs. Rumex, Senicio (more commonly Senecio) and Urtica are each the name of a genus of plants which grow in this country as weeds. The latter is 'arm'd' because the genus Urtica includes the stinging-nettle.

l. 371.   *Darwin*. Erasmus Darwin, the author of a long poem in rhymed couplets, *The Botanic Garden*, the second part of which (published in 1791) was entitled *The Loves of the Plants*. It seems likely that in the whole of this section Crabbe is using Peter Pratt as a stalking-horse for the grandiose pretensions of Darwin himself. The gardener's language reads rather like a not-too-distant parody of Darwin's descriptions of 'floral courtships', while 'simpering' (line 373) would aptly describe the tone of much of *The Loves of the Plants* as well.

l. 394. *And call it science and philosophy.* Cf. the Advertisement to Darwin's *The Botanic Garden*:

The general design of the following sheets is to inlist Imagination under the banner of Science; and to lead her votaries from the looser analogies which dress out the imagery of poetry, to the stricter ones which form the ratiocination of philosophy.

ll. 399, 400. *scaly tribes; plumy people.* Crabbe is here using the conventional circumlocutions of eighteenth-century poetic diction for 'fish' and 'birds' respectively. Both 'scaly' and 'plumy' are adjectives to which Erasmus Darwin is somewhat addicted.

l. 407. *Grew, and Middleton, and Ray.* Neremiah Grew, author of *The Anatomy of Plants*; William Middleton, author of *The Properties of Herbs*; John Ray, author of *Historia Generalis Plantarum*: all distinguished seventeenth-century naturalists.

ll. 410-11. One of the characteristics of the Latitudinarian theology of the eighteenth century was the disposition to regard the scientific study of nature as a means of discovering fresh aspects of the wisdom and benevolence of the Creator.

l. 419. *clown.* Peasant or rustic.

l. 426. *our village-sires.* The eighteenth-century parish was responsible for the support and maintenance not only of its own poor but also of any child born within the parish boundaries, or any foundling discovered there. This responsibility (like all those connected with the poor of the parish) was administered by an annually appointed overseer, and financed out of the parish poor-rate; but it rested ultimately upon the Vestry, the gathering of all the ratepayers of the parish whose deliberations Crabbe here describes. Routine vestry business was often dealt with by a mere handful of the more important or public-spirited parishioners; but for a small parish the discovery of a foundling to be maintained for many years out of the rates would be an event important enough to call for a fully attended meeting—or even, in this case apparently, for a series of such meetings (see line 428).

By what means does Crabbe bring out in these lines the grudging and hard-hearted attitude of the 'village-sires' to their 'unwelcome guest'?

L

l. 470.   *fame*. Reputation.

ll. 473-4.   Richard had reached the age at which he could be bound in apprenticeship by the parish—a fate which he was understandably determined to avoid. (See *The Borough*, Letter XXII; especially lines 59-94 and note.)

l. 476.   *deem'd him hanging*. 'Took the view that he was bound to end up on the gallows.'

l. 480.   *wit*. Mental alertness.

l. 504.   The parallelism between 'bounty' and 'blows' which rounds off the anecdote so neatly has been anticipated in at least three earlier phrases. See if you can locate them.

Notice also the details in the character sketch of Richard as a boy which have prepared us to credit his later worldly success.

l. 544.   *and now his face . . . and now his feet*. Because they were looking for the devil's horns and cloven hoof.

l. 552.   *trepan*. Trick, cheat.

l. 553.   A side hit at Thomas Paine, whose book, *The Rights of Man* (1791), was a defence of the French Revolution against the attack of Crabbe's first patron, Edmund Burke. Though in fact Paine was a Deist whose scorn for organised religion was accompanied by a sincere belief in the God underlying the works of Nature, he was widely attacked by the orthodox as an atheist—a misconception which would make the slighting reference to his book seem more appropriate to the present context than it really is.

ll. 566-9.   Crabbe is here preparing a transition to Part II of his poem—*Marriages*.

ll. 570-1.   'Allusions of this kind are to be found in the *Fairy Queen*. See the end of the first book, and other places.' (Crabbe's note.)

Although the plan of the poem permits the poet to present his individual character-portraits in a wholly random order (the order in which the entries happen to occur in the parish register), there are in fact certain trains of thought which enable Crabbe to lead on naturally from one character to the next. Which character-sketches are connected with each other in this way? To what extent would you justify (on this or any other grounds) the arrangement of topics in this section of the poem? Do you agree with the French critic, M. René Huchon, that the poem is 'deficient in methodical arrangement and unity'?

Page 44   PART III. BURIALS

l. 20.   During the reign of George III the laws against poaching were enforced with increasing severity and savagery, and spring-guns and man-traps were widely used by game-preservers until their prohibition in 1827.

l. 28.   *the night's amusements.* i.e. of poaching.

ll. 29-32.   A reference to the successful suppression by the Evangelical movement of many of the amusements and dissipations which had characterised village life earlier in the eighteenth century. The campaign was launched in 1787 when the King issued a proclamation condemning Sabbath-breaking, blasphemy, drunkenness, obscene literature and immoral amusements; and it was carried on, under Wilberforce's leadership, by the Society for the Reformation of Manners. Even without the aid of legal prohibition by Act of Parliament, the campaign achieved a considerable success in many parts of the country because of the wide arbitrary powers which eighteenth-century custom allowed the local justice of the peace to exercise according to his own discretion.

l. 31.   *justice.* Justice of the peace, or magistrate.

l. 50.   A reference to Edward Young's *Night-Thoughts* (1742-4), a long poem consisting of moralising reflections in blank verse addressed to a fictitious character, Lorenzo. Night I contains the lines :

> Of human ills the last extreme beware,
> Beware, Lorenzo! a low sudden death.

ll. 59-62.   *that great man.* The centurion who appealed to Jesus to heal his servant. See Luke, vii, 8.

ll. 65-72.   In the eighteenth-century countryside the parish was the all-important unit of local government, having responsibility among other things for 'the maintenance of the church and its services, the keeping of the peace, the repression of vagrancy, the relief of destitution, the mending of roads, the suppression of nuisances, the destruction of vermin, the furnishing of soldiers and sailors—even to some extent the enforcing of religious and moral discipline . . .' (S. and B. Webb, *English Local Government*, Vol. I, p. 4.) This 'parish-business' was discharged under the direction of four unpaid Officers of the Parish—the Churchwarden, the Constable, the Surveyor of Highways, and the Overseer of the Poor. In rural parishes the obligation to serve these offices was often attached to certain ancient farms or landholdings, the occupants of which had to fill each of the offices in rotation. If in this way an office fell to a woman, she could always appoint a deputy, but the Widow Goe evidently scorned to do this.

It is as Constable that she would be concerned with the suppression of vagrancy (line 69); as Churchwarden that she would act as a guardian of morals (line 70); and as Overseer of the Poor that she would have to mete out poor relief (lines 71-2). (Since any illegitimate children born in the parish would almost certainly be a burden upon the poor-rate, perhaps it is also in her capacity as overseer that she would be impelled to utter 'her stern rebuke' to the 'pregnant damsels'.)

l. 98. *hinds*. Farm servants.

ll. 101-8. Notice how Crabbe brings out the way in which her mind is divided between spiritual and worldly concerns by his use of balance and antithesis within the couplet or within the individual line.

ll. 113-14. What effect of irony is gained by the repetition of the phrase 'in haste'?

THE BOROUGH

This long poem is in the form of a series of twenty-four letters written by an inhabitant of the borough to a friend living in a distant village. The first letter consists of a 'General Description', and there then follows a group of eleven letters describing particular aspects of the life of the borough, namely: The Church: The Vicar—The Curate, etc.; Sects and Professions in Religion; Elections; Professions—Law; Professions —Physic; Trades; Amusements; Clubs and Social Meetings; Inns; Players. Letter XIII deals with 'The Alms-House and Trustees', and is followed by three letters each telling the story of one of the 'Inhabitants of the Alms-House'—Blaney, Clelia and Benbow. The next letter is entitled 'The Hospital and Governors', and then comes 'The Poor and their Dwellings', followed by the stories of four of the 'Poor of the Borough'— The Parish-Clerk, Ellen Orford, Abel Keene and Peter Grimes. The poem concluded with two more general sections entitled 'Prisons' and 'Schools' respectively.

It should perhaps be mentioned that, although Crabbe's Borough is clearly modelled to a very considerable extent upon Aldeburgh (which it resembles particularly in its scenery and topography), it is not to be regarded as a literal transcription of Crabbe's birthplace; there are differences as well as similarities.

Page 47   LETTER V. THE ELECTION

The English borough is a unit of a government with a history which goes back even beyond the medieval period. In essence, a 'municipal borough' was a township which had acquired certain privileges and rights of self-government, these rights having usually been recognised at some stage by the grant of a Royal Charter. In 1295 certain boroughs were summoned to send two burgesses to Parliament in addition to the two 'knights of the shire' who represented each county there; and the number of these 'Parliamentary boroughs' increased steadily though irregularly over the next three and a half centuries. From the time of the Restoration until the Parliamentary Reform Act of 1832, the members representing the English boroughs constituted numerically by far the largest section of the House of Commons. There were, in fact, no fewer than 197 English Parliamentary boroughs returning two members each, as against 40 English counties with two members each, and 12 Welsh counties and 13 Welsh boroughs with one member each.

During the eighteenth century, however, the boroughs had

also become that part of the electoral system which was most open to abuses of various kinds. For one thing, they had often long ceased to be important centres of population; for another, the franchise was a matter of local custom (which varied greatly from borough to borough) and was often extremely restricted in its basis. Thus, although the parliamentary enfranchisement of the boroughs had originally constituted an extension of representative government, by this period borough elections had become much less genuinely democratic than the elections for the counties, which were on a wider and more uniform franchise.

It should be noted there was (and still is) no necessary connection between a municipal borough and a parliamentary borough. The Borough of Crabbe's poem is, however, clearly both, and in this it resembles its prototype, Aldeburgh, which was granted a Royal Charter as a municipal borough by Henry VIII, and was created a parliamentary borough returning two members by Queen Elizabeth I. The nature of the franchise in Crabbe's Borough is not made explicit in the poem; but we may perhaps suspect that it is not a very wide one, if only because in 1832, when Aldeburgh was wholly disfranchised by the Parliamentary Reform Act, the total number of electors for the borough was only 35. In general, of course, the smaller the number of electors, the greater were the opportunities for corruption.

ll. 1-8. The Englishman's *freedom* to elect his own government was a common patriotic boast, particularly during the Napoleonic wars; and it also provided a campaign-cry for both Whig and Tory parties. In his play upon the word here, Crabbe also introduces other senses, e.g. 'freedom from customary civilised restraints'. Try as far as possible to decide the exact sense or senses present on each occasion. See also lines 21-2, and the note on line 103 below.

l. 28. *noble.* i.e. belonging to one of the aristocratic families from which the overwhelming majority of eighteenth-century parliamentary candidates were drawn.

l. 30. *the little place.* Throughout the eighteenth century all posts in the government, even those of the lowest kind, were obtainable almost exclusively through political influence; and the trading of votes in return for the promise of a 'place' in, say, the Customs and Excise or the Post Office was a commonplace feature of all parliamentary elections.

l. 54. *gibbous back*. Hunchback.

l. 60. *brute-spirit*. Public opinion. Cf the phrase 'Goths and Huns' in line 56, with its suggestion of the barbarous and uncivilised.

l. 64. *nearly guess*. Shrewdly estimate.

l. 69. *start as in a race*. i.e. the race for political influence and advancement.

ll. 93-4. Cf. lines 69-70.

l. 103. *freedom*. i.e. freedom to vote. The 'promotion' has come, of course, through selling this 'freedom' to one of the candidates. Probably Crabbe intends us to understand that in his Borough only the Freemen (i.e. members of the corporation) were entitled to the Parliamentary vote; in which case there is a further play upon the word 'freedom' here. Perhaps the 'smiths and cobblers' in line 5 are also 'free' in this sense.

l. 105. *naughty*. Wicked.

l. 107. *at mighty cost*. Election costs (then subject to no legal restriction) had mounted rapidly during the eighteenth century, and it was not uncommon for a successful candidate to have spent many hundreds of pounds in securing his return.

l. 111. *indulgent lease*. In addition to direct bribery, another form of persuasion open to the candidate who was a land-owner was to renew a tenant-farmer's lease upon unduly favourable terms.

l. 127. *on the victorious part*. Belonging to the victorious side.

l. 134. *broad-cloth*. Originally, a fine, plain-wove, double-width black cloth, used chiefly for men's clothes. Later, the term came to be used to imply quality rather than width.

l. 135. *his seat*. His mayoral seat of office.

l. 136. He continues to wear his blue seaman's suit for everyday purposes.

ll. 137-80. In his Preface to the poem, Crabbe makes the following comment on this episode: 'The circumstance re-corded in the fifth Letter is a fact; although it may appear to many almost incredible, that, in this country, and but a few years since, a close and successful man should be a stranger to the method of increasing money by the loan of it. The Minister of the place where the honest Fisherman resided has related to me the apprehension and suspicion he witnessed: With trembling hand and dubious look, the careful man received and surveyed the bond given to him; and, after a sigh or two of lingering mistrust, he placed it in the coffer whence he had just before taken his cash; for which, and for whose increase, he now indulged a belief, that it was indeed both promise and security.'

l. 140. Crabbe's own note to this reads: 'I am informed that some explanation is here necessary, though I am ignorant for what class of my readers it can be required. Some corporate bodies have actual property, as appears by their receiving rents; and they obtain money on the admission of members into their society: this they may lawfully share perhaps. There are, moreover, other doles, of still greater value, of which it is not necessary for me to explain the nature, or to inquire into the legality.' As this suggests, the corporations were by Crabbe's time notorious for the extent to which their members (and especially their officials) lined their own pockets out of funds and resources originally intended for other purposes (including sometimes valuable charitable endowments, for example). It should perhaps be explained that membership of the corporation (conferring the title of Freeman or Burgess) did not belong to all the inhabitants of a borough, but was a privilege to be procured only on conditions which varied from borough to borough, but usually included a substantial entrance-fee. At Aldeburgh freedom could be acquired only by serving an apprenticeship in the borough or by co-option; and in either case a substantial fee was exacted.

l. 147. *put it out*. Lend it out at interest.

l. 162. *interest*. Daniel so far understands the word only in the sense of 'political interest or influence'.

l. 170. *my late knowledge*. 'My lateness in acquiring knowledge.'

l. 175. *interest*. Crabbe's play upon the word here combines

168

the two senses previously kept separate, together with the further suggestion of 'self-interest'.

l. 177. i.e. Daniel's admission to the corporation in the first instance (as Freeman or Burgess) had been by co-option. See note on line 140 above.

l. 184. *warm*. Politically ardent. See also line 193.

l. 189. *blue and green*. Presumably the local colours of the two political parties. In Norwich around this time the Tory colours were purple and orange, while the Whig colours were blue and white; in Ipswich the rival colours were blue and yellow respectively.

l. 193. *bodger*. A clumsy workman, a botcher.

l. 194. *gains less int'rest*. Carries less influence (in the burgess's choice of his tailor).

ll. 197-201. Crabbe's vindication of British democratic institutions despite their defects is very much in the spirit of the constitutional writings of his first patron, Edmund Burke.

In what ways does the anecdote about the Mayor fit in with the general pattern of argument of this Letter?

Page 53   LETTER XIX. THE PARISH-CLERK

Originally (in pre-Reformation days) the Parish Clerk had ranked among the minor orders of the Church, but by the eighteenth century the office had declined to a position half-way between that of a curate and that of a menial church servant. Though it was usually filled by an uneducated layman, a certain tradition of clerical learning still hung about the office; and this no doubt accounts for the self-importance of Jachin in Crabbe's tale, and also for the tinge of irony in the references to Jachin's own estimate of his learning (see lines 6 and 18, for example).

The name Jachin is itself significant; Jachin and Boaz were the names of the two pillars in the porch of the temple of Solomon (see 1 Kings vii, 21).

In the church service the Parish Clerk led the responses of the congregation, or even in many cases uttered all the responses on their behalf; and he also had a large responsibility for the musical side of the service, for it was his duty 'to give out the Psalm, to lead it, very commonly to read it out line by line, and frequently to select what was to be sung'.

l. 2. *hight*. Named (archaic).

15. *light . . . light*. A play upon the two senses; (*a*) 'frivolous, unthinking'; (*b*) 'trivial, unimportant'.

l. 17. *high seat*. The Parish Clerk usually occupied a seat in church below that of the priest but above the level of the congregation.

ll. 20-1. It is perhaps worth noticing that Jachin's attitude here rather closely resembles that of the over-zealous Evangelical converts in *Advice: or, The 'Squire and the Priest*. (See especially lines 404-11 of the latter Tale.)

l. 25. *pioneer*. In the original military sense, one of the body of soldiers who marched in advance of an army to repair roads and clear the way for the main body.

l. 38. *that*. So that.

l. 38. *in sin's despite*. 'In anger at sin' or 'in punishment of sin'—an older sense of 'despite' than the one mainly current to-day.

l. 51. *a fish who led the fry*. In what ways is this metaphor appropriate to Jachin?

Notice that here (lines 44-51) and in at least two later passages Crabbe himself writes of Satan in terms rather similar to those used by Jachin. What is the tone of these references?

l. 70. *the bold-one*. Satan. Why is it particularly in character for Jachin to use this epithet?

l. 77. *the final feast*. The feast which the candidate provided for his supporters on the day of a Parliamentary election.

l. 86. *'Amen, so be it.'* A sample of the responses in the church service which it was the duty of the Parish Clerk to intone aloud (and to which, in the view of 'Satan' and 'Satan's friends', he ought to confine himself).

l. 113. *engines*. Traps or snares.

l. 127. *weakest*. i.e. in resisting temptation.

The 'burgess' is treated with respect by the 'common herd' because, unlike them, he has acquired the 'freedom of the borough' and is therefore a man of importance.

l. 130. *parts*. Talents, intellectual abilities.

ll. 136-7. A major part of the remuneration of a Parish Clerk consisted of the customary fees for christenings, weddings and funerals which he was entitled to recover from the individual parishioners concerned.

l. 146. *Once in a month*. During the eighteenth century the Holy Communion was seldom celebrated more frequently than once a month, even in large towns; while in country parishes it was a common practice for the celebration to take place only four times a year.

ll. 150-1. Private pews (tall wooden boxes of a shape and size which led Swift to compare them satirically to 'bedsteads of the antique mode') were introduced into most churches during the eighteenth century for the greater comfort of the wealthier members of the congregation.

l. 153. *oblation*. In general, 'something offered to God for pious uses'; but the term is used particularly for the offering made during the Holy Communion service.

ll. 186-8. Notice that it is the perversion of reason (finding arguments to suit one's inclinations) that Crabbe is describing and condemning here. Notice also in line 188 the economy with which Crabbe suggests, by the antithesis between 'quickly' and 'slowly', the strength of Jachin's resistance to temptation.

ll. 189-90. The celebration of the Holy Communion came at the end of the customary Sunday morning service in accordance with the usual eighteenth-century procedure.

l. 204. *thought*. With the meaning of 'had thought'; he had forgotten to take the intended precaution of filling his pocket with bran. What effect does this detail have upon our sympathies?

ll. 211-12. 'Hanoverian churchmen approached the Holy Communion with a sense of awe, and upon occasion with a haunting fear lest unworthy participation should provoke not a blessing but a curse upon them.' (N. Sykes, *Church and State in England in the Eighteenth Century*, p. 277.)

l. 230. *churl*. In the double sense of (*a*) a rude low-bred fellow, and (*b*) one who is hard and miserly in money matters.

l. 230. *overseer.* For information about the parish offices, including that of Overseer of the Poor, see note to lines 65-73 of *The Parish Register*, Part III.

Although the parish offices were supposed, legally, to be filled by 'substantial householders', in practice gentlemen often chose to pay a fine in order to be excused from their turn of duty; and the office of overseer (a particularly onerous and unpleasant one) usually fell on farmers or small tradesmen, who were commonly ill-qualified for their task and often even illiterate. (Notice the word 'lewd' in line 231.) The mean tyrannical overseer, concerned only to keep down the poor-rate to a minimum is a constantly recurring figure in all accounts of eighteenth-century poor-law administration.

l. 231. *lewd.* Unlearned, illiterate. The contrast with the 'learned' Parish Clerk makes Jachin's humiliation at this man's hands even more painful, of course.

l. 234. *the disgrace.* The Holy Communion offering was customarily dedicated to the relief of the poor, and though it was not of course part of the actual poor-rate, the overseer would no doubt be concerned in its distribution. He is angry, therefore, because he considers that suspicion has been cast upon his own honesty.

l. 278. *bounding.* Serving as a boundary between neighbouring estates or parishes.

l. 292. *reason'd.* i.e. rationalised. See lines 187 and 213.

> Thus far the playful Muse has lent her aid,
> But now departs, of graver theme afraid.
>
> (lines 118-19).

What difference of tone do you notice between the earlier and later parts of this letter? Does this difference contribute anything to the total effect of the poem? Pay particular attention to lines 289-96.

Page 61   LETTER XXII. PETER GRIMES

l. 21. *hot spirit.* Presumably rum or gin, both of which were comparatively cheap in the eighteenth century.

l. 32. *settle.* A wooden bench with arms and a high back.

l. 42.   *mark'd.* Noticed or observed.

l. 52.   *various.* Of diverse kinds (compare the account of his thefts in the previous paragraph).

ll. 59-65.   Parish apprenticeship was an inexpensive form of poor relief commonly practised in the London district towards the end of the eighteenth century; even at the time at which Crabbe was writing some 500 to 600 children were bound in this way every year by London parishes.

The children apprenticed by the parish would include foundlings, illegitimate children born within the parish, children maintained in the workhouse, and also the children of those receiving parish doles. The parish overseer's first concern was to bind out the child to a master living in another parish, since after serving an apprenticeship of forty days the apprentice would gain a settlement in the new parish, and whatever happened after that could no longer become a burden upon the rates of his original parish. To secure this end, a fee (of £5 or so) was commonly offered as an inducement to a master who would take a pauper child off the hands of the parish responsible for him and undertake to maintain him and teach him a trade in return for the benefits of his labour. Such apprenticeships were usually to the less skilled and more badly paid trades, and the overseers rarely made any attempt to ensure that the master was a fit person to be responsible for an apprentice. As a consequence, cases were frequently reported of parish apprentices who died as a result of neglect or brutality, and this led in time to protests against the system from social reformers.

It is perhaps of interest that one authority states that 'Fishermen's and watermen's apprentices were notoriously ill-treated.' (M. Dorothy George, *London Life in the Eighteenth Century*, p. 231.)

ll. 79-85.   Try to identify the specific poetic qualities which make this catalogue of ill-treatment so powerful in its effect.

l. 152.   Notice how the order in which the fish and the apprentice are mentioned (and the way in which they share the same verb) underline the callousness of the speaker.

l. 174.   *bounding.* Forming a boundary to the stream.

l. 190. *muscles*. An obsolete spelling of 'mussels'.

l. 208. *reach*. 'The reaches in a river are those parts which extend from point to point. Johnson has not the word precisely in this sense; but it is very common, and I believe used wheresoever a navigable river can be found in this country.' (Crabbe's note.)

l. 234. *glasses*. Telescope.

l. 249. *resign'd*. Abandoned.

l. 252. *distemper'd*. Mentally disordered, insane.

l. 253. *parish-bed*. A bed in the workhouse.

What does Crabbe's careful description of the river-scene (lines 171-204) contribute to the poem?

Crabbe writes in his preface: 'The mind here exhibited (in the character of Peter Grimes) is one untouched by pity, unstung by remorse, and uncorrected by shame.' Compare Jachin and Grimes from the point of view of (*a*) the author's attitude towards them and their crimes, and (*b*) the nature of the retribution which overtakes them.

TALES IN VERSE

Page 71   PROCRASTINATION·

In the 1834 edition, the poet's son and biographer adds the following note to this poem:

'Mr Crabbe's sons have no doubt but that their mother's residence, at one time, with her rich old aunt, who was very partial to her, and abounded in trinkets, suggested this supposition.'

Crabbe first met Sarah Elmy in 1772; throughout their long engagement (for only in 1783 did Crabbe's financial position become secure enough to permit them to marry) his future wife lived at Beccles with her aunt Miss Tovell, who disapproved of the match because of the young man's uncertain prospects. Crabbe seems to have felt strongly about the danger of long engagements, for he returns to this theme on several other occasions.

l. 8. *fondness.* In the eighteenth century this word had a range of meanings slightly different from those current to-day, for the original sense of 'folly, lack of sense or judgment', though dying out, was still found occasionally. At times Crabbe uses the word to imply not simply 'tenderness or affectionate feeling', but rather 'affection or tenderness which is excessive, foolish or unreasoning'. Can you decide, from the paragraph as a whole, to what extent this sense is likely to be present here?

ll. 15-16. Notice that a difference between the two lovers is hinted at even at this early stage by the balancing of 'prudent' against 'kind', and of 'beloved' against 'approved'.

l. 32. *teasing.* Causing distress or vexation. The word does not here imply (as it perhaps would in modern English) that the vexation is of a trivial kind, or that it is caused for the sake of enjoying the victim's discomfiture.

l. 33. The syntax is parallel to that of the preceding line. 'And she, though resenting, boasted to be all resigned.'

l. 41. *fond.* The request is 'fond' because it proceeds from the lovers' affection for each other, and also because it is useless and therefore foolish. Cf. note on line 8 above.

ll. 60-1. Apparently it is the artificial nature of her cough which suggests to the lovers that her last illness is going to be a long one. Notice the ironic contrast between 'long contention' (line 61) and 'this brief delay' (line 56).

l. 77. *tabby vest.* A woman's dress made of striped silk taffeta.

l. 86. *the poison-tree.* A fantastically exaggerated legend about the Upas tree was widely current in England during the Romantic period. 'Upas' was the Malay word for poison, and there is in fact a 'poison tree' found in Java, the juice of which was used by the natives to tip their arrows. Stories about it, partly factual, partly fabulous, had appeared in various European countries from the beginning of the seventeenth century onwards, but had not attracted a great deal of attention until 1783 when George Steevens, Fellow of the Royal Society and of the Society of Antiquaries, published a lurid but circumstantial account of it in the *London Magazine*, apparently as a hoax. This account Erasmus Darwin took up quite seriously, and repeated with romantic embellishments in his poem *The*

Loves of the Plants (1791). In his notes to the poem he states: 'There is a poison tree in the Island of Java, which is said by its effluvia to have depopulated the country for twelve or fourteen miles round the place of its growth. . . . Not only animals of all kinds, both quadrupeds, fish and birds, but all kinds of vegetables also are destroyed by the effluvia of the noxious tree; so that in a district of twelve or fourteen miles round it, the face of the earth is quite barren and rocky intermixed only with the skeletons of men and animals, affording a scene of melancholy beyond what poets have described or painters have delineated.' This sensational legend appealed to the imagination of a number of the Romantic poets, including Byron (see *Childe Harold's Pilgrimage*, Canto IV), Southey (see *Thalaba*, Book IX, first edition d. 1800), and Coleridge (who planned a poem about the tree, but never wrote it); while Blake made rather freer but much more impressive use of the theme in two poems in *Songs of Experience* ('The Human Abstract' and 'The Poison Tree'). It is wholly characteristic of Crabbe to use this highly coloured piece of Romantic poetic machinery to illustrate, quite unemotionally, a traditional eighteenth-century moral generalisation.

l. 103.   *changed her book*. Took to reading a different kind of literature. Cf. lines 30-1 and 156-7.

l. 104.   *for*. Instead of.

l. 105.   *Rupert's friend*. Notice the economy with which Crabbe presents the cooling of her affections in terms of this detail of the changed ending to her letters.

l. 108.   *oppressed*. i.e. by her illness.

ll. 110-19.   What is the nature of the irony in this passage? How does it contribute to the effect of the tale as a whole?

l. 118.   *their fondness*. The dead couple's devotion to each other.

ll. 124-5.   She had inherited not only the widow's estate, but also her taste, etc.

l. 133.   *more*. i.e. more willing.

l. 167.   *By hope presented*. Presumably by some would-be suitor, or by a friend who hoped to be remembered in her will as a result.

l. 195. Can you trace the specific details whereby Crabbe has previously displayed the progressive change in Dinah's feelings, stage by stage?

l. 218-19. Notice how this detail prepares us for the calculated insincerity of Dinah's next remarks.

l. 229. Here and later Crabbe catches admirably the bluff frank openness of the sailor's speech.

l. 231. Notice her misinterpretation of Rupert's last remark, and what it tells us of the change in her own values.

l. 244. *other spousal.* i.e. as a 'bride of Christ' in the kingdom of heaven.

l. 247. *the change.* The transition to old age, death and the next world.

l. 254. *spouse.* Used here in the sense not of 'wife' but of 'solemnly betrothed fiancée'.

l. 256. *this.* The fact that the normal rôles of 'giving' and 'taking' would be reversed.

l. 266. *trimmer.* Smarter or more handsome. The natural word for a sailor to use, because of its original application to ships. Cf. line 264.

l. 266. *spark.* In the double sense of (*a*) suitor, and (*b*) man of fashion.

l. 275. *trepann'd.* Cheated, swindled. The suggestion seems to be that he was deceived by false promises from the employer on whose behalf he has worked and worn out his health abroad. Cf. lines 52-3 and 71.

ll. 306, 310. *shares a parish-gift; thick-set coat of badgeman's blue.* Since the beginning of the seventeenth century each parish had been responsible for the support and maintenance of its own poor. This poor-relief was financed by a poor-rate, and administered by an annually appointed overseer, under the supervision of the local magistrates. It took various forms at different times and places, but the 'parish-gift' would probably be a small money-pension or dole, perhaps supplemented by gifts in kind (the 'thick-set coat' sounds like a uniform of coarse cloth supplied by the parish). An Act of 1697 required those in receipt of relief to 'openly wear upon the shoulder of the right sleeve a badge or mark with a large Roman P, and the first letter of the name of the parish . . . cut thereon either in red or blue cloth'. Thus, whatever the precise form of the 'badge-man's blue', it would be the recognised insignia of a pauper who was 'on the parish'.

l, 316. *meaning face*. A face whose expression is con-sciously calculated for the sake of its effect on others.

l. 346. *the Levite*. In the parable of the Good Samaritan (Luke x, 30-37). What is the effect of this New Testament allusion upon our attitude towards Dinah? Why does it make an appropriate and telling conclusion to the poem?

'Nothing can be more forcible or true to nature than the description of the effect of this cold-blooded cant on the warm and unsuspecting nature of her disappointed suitor' (Jeffrey). Does this comment on lines 216-303 seem to you justified?

Page 81   THE FRANK COURTSHIP

l. 35. *An independent race*. The Kindred family are depicted as belonging to one of the old-established Dissenting sects which played a leading part in the Puritan Revolution of Cromwell's time. The Independents (or Congregationalists) were one of the 'three old denominations' of the Civil War period which had in common an acute consciousness of sin, an austere distrust of all worldly pleasure, and a conviction that salvation can only come from Grace, i.e. from the direct revelation of God to the individual soul. Where they differed from the other two 'old denominations' (Presbyterians and Baptists) was in their stress upon the autonomy and self-government of each local body of believers, and in their insist-ence that, in order fully to carry out the will of God as revealed to its members by Grace, each such 'church' must be free of all external human control.

After the Restoration of the Stuarts in 1660, these sects were severely repressed, and the restrictions upon them continued in a modified form even after the Revolution of 1688. As late as the end of the eighteenth century Dissenters were still excluded from the Universities and disqualified from taking any part in civic life, though the legal restrictions upon them were gradually being relaxed in practice. Under these conditions of semi-legal toleration the sects continued to maintain their own life rather apart from that of the community as a whole, but their religion hardened into a strict and austere observance of outward forms from which much of the original inner fire had gone.

In this passage as a whole (lines 33-78), what indications can you find of Crabbe's attitude towards the sect? What contribution do the words 'crew' (line 33) and 'party-rhymes' (line 42) make towards defining this attitude?

l. 39. Oliver Cromwell was himself an Independent in religion. When Crabbe refers to the Independents as 'saints' he is in fact only using a term which had been applied to them in the time of Cromwell's Protectorate, mainly of course by their opponents.

l. 46. The Dissenting sects drew much of their strength from the merchant and shopkeeper class, so that it is characteristic that Jonas Kindred should be a prosperous merchant owning a family business of long standing.

ll. 57-64. In a footnote to the 1834 edition, Crabbe's son vouched for the authenticity of this episode depicting the Independents in front of their secretly preserved portrait of Cromwell: 'Such was the actual consolation of a small knot of Presbyterians [*sic*] in a country town, about sixty years ago.'

ll. 56-62. The reference is to the Protector Cromwell's repeated conflicts with various different Parliaments between 1653 and 1658, in the course of which he excluded recalcitrant or unacceptable members and dismissed the session before the appointed time.

In what respects is it implied that Jonas Kindred resembles his hero Cromwell?

l. 70. *modest*. Probably the primary meaning here is 'scrupulously chaste in language, feeling and conduct', since the word in this sense (originally confined to women) had come in the eighteenth century to be used of men as well. It may also have the additional meaning (the more common one in modern English) of 'diffident or unassuming'; if so, Crabbe presumably intends it ironically. Cf. line 13.

l. 72. *fail'd*. Gone bankrupt.

Notice that the balancing of 'fail'd' and 'gone astray' in this line ironically underlines the way in which the 'saints' were inclined to equate financial and moral worth.

l. 81. *sables*. A poetical term for black mourning garments.

l. 108. *light vocations*. Habitual occupations of a trivial or frivolous kind.

l. 117. *meeting*. Prayer-meeting.

l. 130. *vestal*. A pure-minded chaste virgin. In this sense the word is a standard piece of eighteenth-century poetic diction.

l. 141. *when franks could be procured*. Until the introduction of the cheap penny post in 1839, postal charges (which were based on mileage covered) were extremely expensive—evidently too expensive for the frugal Kindred family. However, local postal officials (the 'clerks of the road') and all members of both Houses of Parliament were allowed to 'frank' letters for free delivery by writing their signatures on the corner of the envelope. By an Act of 1764 each peer or M.P. was entitled to frank ten letters a day and to receive fifteen, and the privilege was not confined to letters actually written by or to the member; as a result it is said that at the end of the eighteenth century the Post Office had to carry about one-tenth of its mail for nothing.

ll. 149-50. 'Her care retained her late husband's wealth for her son (the "one tall youth").'

l. 155. *drab*. Cloth of a dull brown colour. In the late eighteenth century it was customary for men to wear brightly coloured clothing. The young man's drab is therefore an outward sign of his membership of a dissenting sect, as is also his broad-brimmed Puritan hat, and the absence of powder on his 'brown locks'.

ll. 174-85. At this period it was still usual for a marriage to be arranged by parents largely as an alliance between financial equals. The bargaining between Jonas and the widow would be principally over the size of the dowry which the father was to provide with his daughter when she married.

l. 186. *ask'd his daughter*. Asked for his daughter to be sent back home.

l. 196. *preferment*. Promotion to a higher status.

l. 197. She thought, 'What a woman they now esteem me!' Sir Adolphus Ward's emendation from 'what' to 'that' seems unnecessary.

l. 214. *laid*. Attributed.

ll. 214-5. What were the conflicting feelings within Sybil which her aunt misinterpreted?

l. 220. *fondness*. Cf. note on line 8 of *Procrastination*.

l. 233. *ductile*. Tractable, easily led. Do you think Sybil was, in fact, ductile?

l. 236. *gaping*. Yawning (out of boredom).

l. 238. *mock forms*. i.e. her drawing and sketching. Notice the Puritan disapproval of art and novel-reading as frivolous and worldly.

l. 245. *You shall advise the maiden*. What kind of advice did Jonas expect his wife to give Sybil? What would he have thought of the way in which she actually carried out this command?

l. 301. *reason's self*. Notice that even in this extravagant speech Sybil implicitly recognises the authority of reason. Cf. lines 133-4.

l. 373. *that surprise*. The surprise referred to in line 370.

l. 376. *light*. Josiah's reproach is directed partly at the fashionable shape of Sybil's dress, low-cut but full-skirted (see line 382); and partly at the thinness of its material, probably one of the newly introduced washable fabrics such as India muslin. Whereas rich dark shades had been the only practicable colours for women's dress when they were made of stiff heavy satins or brocade, white and soft pale colours had come into fashion with the new materials; so that 'light' may be appropriate to the colour of Sybil's dress as well.

l. 392. *naughty malice*. Both these words have a stronger sense here than in modern English.

l. 414. *Speak'st thou at meeting?*. I.e. Are you in the habit of speaking at prayer-meetings? It seems clear that within this sect the privilege of speaking or testifying was not confined to the minister or even to the elders, though perhaps it would be unusual for the younger members of the congregation to thrust themselves forward in this way.

l. 427. *decent habit with a scarlet dye.* Suitable and becoming clothes of a fashionably bright colour. 'Decent' here means not merely 'respectable' in the modern rather lukewarm sense, but, more positively, 'fitting to one's position'.

l. 430. *long-skirted.* Towards the end of the eighteenth century, long full-skirted frock coats for men gave way to cut-away tail coats; so that in this respect too Josiah's clothes are rather ostentatiously out of fashion.

ll. 442-5. The balance struck here is the essential point of the poem. Notice particularly that each accepts the need to make allowance for the other's point of view and in fact to compromise. Compare the outcome of this discussion with the result of the earlier battle between their respective parents (lines 174-85).

l. 450. *lost in his retreat.* Having lost his way while going out.

l. 491. *That is of grace.* That answer is a sign of spiritual grace or inner illumination. It is characteristic, perhaps, that Jonas uses the old Puritan phrase in an almost conventional way to indicate his own approval (confidently assuming, of course, that the Divine purpose coincides with his own). In line 494, however, his daughter teasingly takes up the phrase's serious significance.

In his article in the *Edinburgh Review*, Jeffrey made the following comment on this poem: '*The Frank Courtship* is rather in the merry vein; and contains even less than Mr Crabbe's usual moderate allowance of incident. The whole of the story is, that the daughter of a rigid Quaker, having been educated from home, conceives a slight prejudice against the ungallant manners of the sect, and is prepared to be very contemptuous and uncomplying when her father proposes a sober youth of the persuasion for a husband; but is so much struck with the beauty of his person, and the cheerful reasonableness of his deportment, at their first interview, that she instantly yields her consent.' What important elements in the poem are omitted from this brief account of it? Can you decide where the poet's sympathy lies as between (*a*) Jonas and Sybil (*b*) Sybil and Josiah? From this poem can you decide whether

Crabbe considers 'love' or 'esteem' the more satisfactory basis on which to commence married life?

Page 96   ARABELLA

l. 1. *guide*. Spiritual guide (i.e. vicar).

l. 23. *above her sex's dread*. During the first half of the eighteenth century, Englishwomen, even those of the upper class, had little education, and were in general content to be treated as intellectually inferior to men. Thus it was considered 'unbecoming' for them to know Greek or Latin, and almost immodest for them to be authors. In the 1750's a small group of society ladies (notably Mrs Vesey and Mrs Montagu) rebelled against this prevailing attitude; they started the practice of giving fashionable evening assemblies to which the only men invited were authors and savants, and took to studying seriously subjects which had hitherto been reserved for men. As a result they acquired the half-malicious title of 'blue-stockings'—a term the origin of which is not altogether certain, but which first appeared about this time. Arabella's accomplishments, as set forth in this paragraph, are those of a typical 'blue-stocking' of the period.

l. 28. *Berkley, Bacon, Hobbes and Locke*. Bishop George Berkeley (1685-1753), Lord Francis Bacon (1561-1626), Thomas Hobbes (1588-1679), and John Locke (1632-1704) were all serious (and difficult) writers on philosophical subjects.

l. 30. *the moral muse*. Clio, the muse of history. For the eighteenth century the main purpose of historical writing was to draw moral lessons and rules for conduct from the experience of the past; hence the close connection between the 'historical' and the 'moral' glanced at here.

l. 31. *the Roman page*. i.e. Latin.

l. 32. *And could converse with Moore and Montagu*. Mrs Elizabeth Robinson Montagu (1720-1800) and Mrs Hannah More (1745-1833) were both prominent members of the original generation of blue-stockings. Both were authors: Mrs Montagu's essay on Shakespeare (1769) was published anonymously, but the authorship was an open secret even at the time; while Mrs More, having gained fame as a verse-writer and dramatist during the 1770's, later turned to writing moral tales and religious tracts on behalf of the Evangelical movement, the most famous of which, *Coelebs in Search of a Wife*, appeared in 1809.

In their evening assemblies the early 'blue-stockings' consciously set out to raise the standard of conversation at mixed social gatherings. Crabbe's line means that in the art of conversation Arabella was accomplished enough to hold her own even with Mrs More and Mrs Montagu; she could, in fact, converse to equal the best of them.

l. 44. *peccant.* Offending or sinning.

l. 68. *spurious offspring.* Illegitimate children.

l. 110. *her mind in balance hung.* Notice how this judicial balancing and 'weighing' (see line 115) of qualities is enacted in the movement of the next three lines (111-13).

It is perhaps worth noticing that each of the first four suitors comes progressively nearer to satisfying Arabella's exacting requirements. When you have read the Tale as a whole, you should try to decide what relationship this has to the central theme of the poem.

l. 155. *fondly.* See note on *Procrastination*, line 8.

l. 160. *slight.* Treat as unimportant.

l. 175. *Forbid it spirit, prudence, virtuous pride.* Notice carefully the motives which lead Arabella to reject Huntly. Examine the rest of this speech for evidence which throws further light on their true nature, and also for any indications of the author's attitude towards them. (See also lines 182-3.)

l. 189. *maiden vot'ress.* A woman devoted to chastity.

l. 193. *over-nice.* Over-particular.

l. 194. *the false sublime.* This phrase shows very clearly the basis of Crabbe's cautious distrust of exalted notions and ardent feelings: unless founded securely on reason they are peculiarly likely to turn out to be misplaced or to lead us into insincerity. For his Romantic contemporaries the word 'sublime' set the seal of approval upon any feeling to which it was applied. Crabbe uses it several times, but almost always with a qualifying adjective. Cf. *Silford Hall*, line 169, 'obscure-sublime'.

l. 201. *venal turn-coat.* One who has changed his political allegiance as a result of being bribed. The buying of votes was an openly accepted feature of elections throughout the eighteenth century, and persisted well into the nineteenth century, even after the Great Reform Bill of 1832. Cf. *The Borough*, Letter V.

l. 203. *his*. i.e. the turn-coat's.

ll. 212-25. Notice the tolerant balance achieved in this passage (in which Crabbe explicitly rejects the easy cynicism of lines 210-11). The closing couplet (lines 224-5) expresses the essential attitude of the poem as a whole, an attitude which is reiterated in the poet's own note at the end of the Tale.

l. 225. *so*. So long as.

ll. 266-75. Cf. lines 186-7.

l. 275. *naughty*. Wicked.

l. 314-15. In the earlier part of the eighteenth century there had been considerable uncertainty about the legal position of negro slaves who had been brought to England by their masters: in 1772, their situation was clarified by the decision (in the famous Somersett case) that 'as soon as any slave sets his foot upon English territory he becomes free'.

ll. 335-7. Notice the pointed contrast between these lines and lines 177-9.

Do you consider that, if read with reasonable care, the Tale offers any grounds for the kind of misunderstanding which Crabbe felt it necessary to guard against in his footnote?

Page 106   THE LOVER'S JOURNEY

In the biography, Crabbe's son comments: 'It was in his walks between Aldeburgh and Beccles that Mr Crabbe passed through the very scenery described in the first part of *The Lover's Journey*; while near Beccles, in another direction, he found the contrast of rich vegetation introduced in the latter part of that tale . . .', and he goes on to express his own conviction that 'the disappointment of the story' refers to an actual experience of his father during one of his visits to Beccles as a young man to see his future wife, Sarah Elmy. Even if this conjecture is correct, it is clear that Crabbe was only making use of his own experience in order to illustrate and develop (from his own rather different point of view) a theme which formed one of the preoccupations of the first generation of Romantic poets: namely, the extent to which the perception of natural beauty is dependent upon the subjective frame of mind of the beholder. The most characteristic Romantic statement of the theme is perhaps to be found in the following stanza from Coleridge's *Dejection: an Ode* (which had first appeared in the *Morning Post* in 1802):

> O Lady! we receive but what we give,
> And in our life alone does Nature live:
> Ours is her wedding garment, ours her shroud!
> And would we aught behold, of higher worth,
> Than that inanimate cold world allowed
> To the poor loveless ever-anxious crowd,
> Ah! from the soul itself must issue forth
> A light, a glory, a fair luminous cloud
> Enveloping the Earth—
> And from the soul itself must there be sent
> A sweet and potent voice, of its own birth,
> Of all sweet sounds the life and element!

l. 2. *descries*. Perceives, observes.

l. 8. *peculiar*. 'Characteristic to themselves alone.'

ll. 10-11. In what ways does the statement made here differ from that made in the first two lines of the Coleridge stanza quoted above? Pay particular attention to the effect of the two words emphasised by the rhyme-scheme—'attend' and 'lend'.

ll. 22-5. Laura was the name by which Petrarch, the fourteenth-century Italian poet, addressed the unknown woman who inspired his long series of love-poems. As a young man Crabbe had himself followed the same convention by assigning the name of 'Mira' to Sarah Elmy in various poems and letters he addressed to her.

l. 27. *fond*. See note on *Procrastination*, line 8.

l. 38. *ling*. Heather.

l. 40. *cup-moss*. A kind of lichen.

l. 42. *herbage*. Grass or other low-growing vegetation.

l. 49. *bounds*. Boundary.

l. 55. *suckling*. A Suffolk word (now obsolete) for honey-suckle or woodbine.

l. 56. *wholesome wormwood*. It is no doubt his joyful feeling of expectancy which leads Orlando to apply this adjective to 'wormwood' which is known to most of us only for its pro-verbial bitter taste; but he had in fact the justification that the tips and leaves of the plant are used in medicine as a tonic.

l. 63. *a common pasture*. Prior to enclosure, there were three types of 'common' around the most typical eighteenth-century village: the common arable field, and the common meadow-land (both of which, though cultivated communally, were divided into strips with different owners), and the common or waste on which all the villagers had the right to pasture cattle, sheep or poultry. In Suffolk the arable and meadowland had been enclosed rather early, much of it even before the begin-ning of the eighteenth century; but as late as 1798 there remained in the county as a whole approximately 100,000 acres of unenclosed waste, mostly of the poor and barren kind which Crabbe describes here.

l. 67. *blacklegs*. A slang term (fairly new in Crabbe's day) for race-course swindlers or sharpers.

ll. 68-9. The 'scattered hovels' would be those of 'squatters' (or 'borderers') who had built themselves huts and cleared a piece of land on the waste at some distance from the village, where their encroachment would usually be tolerated, even though they had strictly no legal claim to their settlement. The cutting of turf from the common for use as fuel was one of the rights or customary privileges which were lost to villagers and squatters alike as a result of enclosure.

l. 71. *sear*. Dry, withered.

l. 72. *wright*. Joiner or carpenter.

l. 74. *'squire*. Lover or gallant.

ll. 74-97. Notice the contrast between Crabbe's realistic portrayal of the scene and the lover's idealising vision of it.

l. 109. *straiten'd*. Confined to a narrow channel.

l. 116. *Flora*. The plants native to the region, personified here as the Roman goddess of flowers.

'The ditches of a fen so near the ocean are lined with

irregular patches of a coarse and stained lava; a muddy sediment rests on the horse-tail and other perennial herbs, which in part conceal the shallowness of the stream; a fat-leaved pale-flowering scurvy-grass appears early in the year, and the razor-edged bull-rush in the summer and autumn. The fen itself has a dark and saline herbage; there are rushes and *arrow-head*, and in a few patches the flakes of the cotton-grass are seen, but more commonly the *sea-aster*, the dullest of that numerous and hardy genus; a *thrift*, blue in flower, but withering and remaining withered till the winter scatters it; the *saltwort*, both simple and shrubby; a few kinds of grass changed by their soil and atmosphere, and low plants of two or three denominations undistinguished in a general view of the scenery;—such is the vegetation of the fen when it is at a small distance from the ocean; and in this case there arise from it effluvia strong and peculiar, half-saline, half-putrid, which would be considered by most people as offensive, and by some as dangerous; but there are others to whom singularity of taste or association of ideas has rendered it agreeable and pleasant.' (Crabbe's note.)

Notice how the poet's botanical learning and interests are also apparent in the minutely accurate observation and description of natural scenery running through the whole poem.

l. 122. *sallows.* A shrubby low-growing species of willow.

l. 122. *septfoil.* Tormentil, a trailing plant with small yellow flowers, common on heaths.

l. 123. *mallow.* A common wild plant, with hairy stems and leaves, and a very sticky sap.

l. 127. *a wat'ry tribe.* i.e. sea-birds. A reminder of conventional eighteenth-century poetic diction in which it was quite customary to refer to birds in general as 'the feathered tribe'.

l. 133. *nice.* Attentive, searching into minute details.

l. 136. *sweet myrtle of the shaking ground.* Bog myrtle (as opposed to common myrtle).

l. 141. *Again the country was enclosed.* He has come to the end of the stretch of common. Cf. line 63.

l. 160. *offended.* Shocked, morally displeased.

l. 163. *fences.* Hedges.

l. 176. *with such.* i.e. with such a look.

l. 181. *intruding*. An expression of the old woman's attitude towards her grandchildren (whom she stints of their fair share of food).

l. 196. *But this Orlando felt not*. Notice that here Orlando's feelings have led him not merely into idealising a landscape, but into an insensibility which misjudges the moral aspect of human character and conduct.

l. 229. *slight*. Treat with indifference or disrespect.

ll. 232-63. Notice, again, the contrast between Crabbe's description of the objective reality of the scene and the lover's vision of it.

l. 283. *seduce*. In the double sense of (*a*) win over by charm and attractiveness, and (*b*) lead astray into a mistaken view of life.

l. 297. *spleen*. i.e. the angry Orlando. Cf. line 45.

l. 304. The inversion serves to emphasise the prophecy. 'And as for these cheerful friends, they will behold. . . .'

ll. 323-4. 'Don't be upset to find that the woman whose love you're so proud of is in great demand as a guest.'

l. 346. *but appeared to die*. Only appeared in order to die away immediately.

'It is the soul that sees.' Despite this stated theme, there are certain features of the poem which tend to suggest that what the soul sees is, in fact, an illusion. Can you identify these features? How important a part should they play in our total response to the poem?

Does this Tale seem to you to justify 'the assertion that in the use of description, of nature and the environment generally, for emotional purposes, Crabbe surpasses any Romantic'? (The quotation contained in this question is taken from F. R. Leavis, *Revaluation*, p. 128.)

Page 116 ADVICE; or, THE 'SQUIRE AND THE PRIEST

In reading this Tale it is as well to be aware that it had been not at all uncommon during the eighteenth century for English clergymen to display the lax worldliness and subservience which the 'Squire expects of a rector who holds the living under his patronage. The intimate dependence of the Anglican clergy upon the governing class of this time was well summarised in Adam Smith's contemporary observation that they 'naturally endeavour to recommend themselves to the sovereign, to the court, and to the nobility and gentry of the country, by whose influence they chiefly expect to obtain preferment'. (*Wealth of Nations*, III, p. 234.) The Methodist and Evangelical movements, which were closely allied in their earlier phase, were a protest against the want of spiritual depth and fervour which characterised this kind of Latitudinarian churchmanship. Their influence was at first felt most widely among the lower and middle classes, and only gradually extended upwards to affect the manners and morals of the landed gentry. Crabbe's Tale typifies their impact, towards the end of the century, upon the last citadels of the older order.

l. 7.   *in travel*. It was customary for an eighteenth-century gentleman to complete his education by a 'Grand Tour' of several European countries.

l. 28.   *son*. Son of the Church (or clergyman).

l. 41.   *bigot*. Strictly, a person obstinately and unreasonably attached to a particular religious opinion; but the word is clearly used here as a term of abuse, with a range of reference similar to that of the term 'Methody'. (Cf. the 'Squire's reference to 'Methodists' in line 73.) The Methodist movement drew many of its preachers, as well as most of its supporters, from the lower classes; and it seems that the word 'bigot' here carries particularly the suggestion of an *uneducated* religious zealot (as contrasted with the university-trained 'man of parts' of line 43).

l. 45.   *where no one dares reply*. i.e. from the pulpit.

l. 48.   *a patriot's zeal*. Perhaps because of the feeling among the upper classes, after the French Revolution, that churchgoing had become a patriotic duty, as a defence against 'godless' Jacobinism.

l. 52.   *place*. The 'Squire evidently had the presentation of this living within his own gift. In about half the parishes of England and Wales the appointment of the vicar was at this period in the hands of one of the large land-owning families.

l. 66.   *tithe*. The tenth part of the annual product of all the farm-land in the parish, which was set aside for the support of the clergyman.

l. 66.   *glebe*. The land assigned to a clergyman as part of his benefice.

l. 87.   *form the very guide*. 'Train exactly the kind of clergyman.'

l. 88.   *decent abroad*. 'Behaving, in his public life, in a way fitting to a clergyman.'

l. 90.   *specious*. Fair-seeming, plausible (but in reality fallacious).

l. 93.   *clerks*. Clerics.

l. 100.   The preacher who influenced James seems to have been based upon Charles Simeon (1759-1836), the Cambridge clergyman and leading Evangelical churchman who over a long period gathered round him at Cambridge a large following of devoted young men upon whom he exercised a far-reaching influence.

l. 100.   *stray'd*. In what respects is this word appropriate here?

l. 103.   *specious*. Attractive in appearance.

l. 106.   *pliant*. Cf. line 59. By what means has the poet prepared us to accept as credible the 'fixing' of James' 'pliant will'?

l. 113.   *subdue*. Perhaps in the double sense of (*a*) make submissive to God, and (*b*) gain control over.

l. 114.   *ghostly*. Spiritual.

l. 116.   *stout*. Healthy, robust.

l. 134.   *the foe*. i.e. the gout.

l. 139.   *revoke*. Change his attitude, go back on what he had said in his sermons.

l. 165.   *essay*. Trial, testing.

ll. 174-262.   The style of preaching recommended by the 'Squire is, in fact, the one which was most widely practised during the eighteenth century, until the Methodist and Evangelical movements brought back a note of fervour into the pulpit. Even Dr Johnson, himself a warm supporter of the Established Church, took the view that its sermons were often

above the heads of the congregation, saying that 'the established clergy in general did not preach plain enough; the
polished periods and glittering sentences flew over the heads of
the common people without any impression on their hearts'.
In their content, moreover, Latitudinarian sermons undoubtedly tended to make the demands of the Christian religion as
little exacting as possible.

l. 187.   *the rubrick*. The directions for the conduct of divine
service, printed in the prayer-book.

l. 201.   *confiding*. Trusting. Said perhaps with a side-glance
at his mistress?

l. 202.   *all embracing*. 'If all were to embrace it.'

l. 211.   *clown*. Ignorant, uneducated countryman.

l. 221.   *failing*. i.e. failing in his religious and moral
obligations.

l. 232.   *tropes and figures*. Rhetorical figures of speech.

ll. 248-55.   If the attitude expressed in these lines seems too
barefacedly cynical to be at all credible, it should be remembered that an eighteenth-century reader would hardly have
found it so. See, for instance, Fielding's account of Parson
Supple in *Tom Jones* (especially Book VI, Chapter IX).

l. 289.   *partial*. Prejudiced (in favour of his protégé).

l. 295.   *grace*. The Evangelical party within the Anglican
Church belonged in a general way to the Calvinist tradition
with its stress upon justification by 'faith' rather than 'works';
thus the choice of a text dealing with 'the power of grace' made
it clear that the sermon was to be an Evangelical one. Cf. the
'Squire's warning against 'that gloomy faith' (lines 194-7).

ll. 309-12.   Notice that in manner as well as matter the
sermon is completely at variance with what the 'Squire had
enjoined.

l. 323.   *fix'd*. Cf. note on line 106.

l. 328.   *parent*. Kinsman (possibly with the additional sense
of sponsor or protector).

l. 330.   *nice*. Discriminating.

l. 340.   'The doubtful (cost him) fear. . . .'

l. 347.   *the third bottle*. An instance of the proverbial heavy
drinking which was habitual among the eighteenth-century

aristocracy. The typical hunting squire would drink claret, burgundy or Rhenish with his dinner, and then port or madeira with the dessert, spending long hours over the latter, and often consuming as much as three or four bottles in an evening. In this case the drinking companions have only reached the stage of opening the third bottle.

l. 347. *spirit*. Aroma.

l. 348. Presumably they are drinking toasts to former cronies.

l. 350. *start*. Show fear.

ll. 361-72. Notice how skilfully Crabbe catches the fuddled incoherence of the man's speech. Cf. lines 357-8.

l. 390. *compound*. Satisfy a duty or obligation by some easier substitute, frequently a money payment: a common eighteenth-century word for a common eighteenth-century practice.

'Crabbe, who, if indubitably a good parson, is a good eighteenth-century parson, holds the balance, in reason's name, between the old profligate and the young zealot, the uncompromising moralist who makes social decency and civilised order impossible' (F. R. Leavis).

Examine the poem as a whole (and especially from line 334 to the end) for evidence which will enable you to decide whether or not Crabbe does in fact hold the balance exactly even.

Page 128   THE WAGER

Crabbe prefixed each of the Tales with a series of Shakespearean quotations which, in general, have been omitted from the present edition. Those belonging to this Tale are included, however, both as a sample of Crabbe's practice in this respect and because they suggest that the poet had consciously taken the idea for his Tale from the last act of '*The Taming of the Shrew*'.

l. 1. *men in trade*. Merchants.

ll. 1-2. *pains/Credit and prudence*. Their steady prosperity is thus due to their painstaking habits of work; their reputation for solvency and fair-dealing (so that people were prepared to trust them with loans of money or with goods 'on credit'); and their cautious business acumen. It should be remembered that banking facilities were limited and local in the eighteenth century, and that business was normally conducted on a credit basis, by means of 'bills' or promissory notes which changed hands almost in the way that paper money does to-day. Consequently a merchant's 'credit' had then both a much greater practical significance and a more specific meaning.

l. 3. *punctual.* Prompt in delivering goods or paying debts.

l. 5. *When they had fix'd some little time in life.* When they had been established in a secure position in life for some time.

l. 29. *nice.* Particular, fastidious.

l. 33. *affect.* Pretend.

ll. 62-3. Compare these lines with lines 46-7, and notice how in each case the rhythm and movement of the couplet fits and underlines the action and attitude it describes.

l. 65. *its.* Notice the colloquial use of the impersonal pronoun, as if she were a baby. Why is this effective here?

In this paragraph as a whole, it is worth noticing Crabbe's ability to achieve a conversational ease and fluency within the strict framework of the heroic couplet.

l. 67. *stove.* A hothouse for plants.

l. 78. *no affairs she knew.* She had no knowledge of or opinions about public affairs. Cf. 'state-affairs' in line 106.

l. 85. *sped.* 'Succeeded in my purpose.'

l. 97. *neighbours . . . neighbouring.* This is an example of the rather pointless and mechanical playing upon words in which Crabbe occasionally indulges. See the parody from the *Rejected Addresses* reprinted on pp. 199-202.

ll. 110-22. Notice the acute psychological observation displayed in Crabbe's insight into the motives underlying Counter's boastfulness; though he would not think in terms of 'unconscious motivation', he is aware of the complexity of human behaviour and interested in its 'unreasonable' elements.

l. 154. *pleasant.* Jocular, merry (perhaps including the now rare sense of 'hilarious as a result of drink').

l. 156. *recreant.* Cowardly or faint-hearted, and also likely to want to go back on his word. ·

ll. 194-202. Why has Crabbe chosen to report this particular speech in the third person? Does this method of presentation help to suggest the diplomatic and indirect approach which Counter feels is necessary?

l. 242. *accent querulous*. Notice how this description sums up a quality which we have already been made aware of in the tone and rhythm of her previous speeches.

ll. 283-91. In what respects is the image of 'weeping willows' particularly appropriate to the argument here? What aspect which is missing from this metaphor does the comparison with ice (line 290) supply?

Can you trace the way in which Crabbe differentiates the characters of the four principals in this story by their actual manner of speech? See particularly the various conversations from line 163 onwards.

POSTHUMOUS TALES

Page 137 SILFORD HALL; or, THE HAPPY DAY

This poem seems to have been founded upon Crabbe's own boyhood visits, when an apothecary's apprentice, to Cheveley, a mansion belonging to the same Duke of Rutland to whom the poet later became domestic chaplain.

l. 2. *of small resort*. Little frequented.

ll. 11-12. Nathaniel Perkin apparently kept one of the small eighteenth-century village schools to which farmers and others would send their children at the cost of a few pence per week. Such schools (like the 'dame schools' kept by elderly women) confined themselves for the most part to the teaching of reading and writing.

l. 29. *yeoman*. A farmer who cultivated his own land.

l. 29. *peevish*. Perverse or spiteful.

ll. 32-3. Nathaniel thus included among his duties those of parish clerk (see note to *The Borough*, Letter XIX). His 'seat below' (line 33) was perhaps the clerk's desk in one of the old three-decker pulpits, with the reader's desk and the preacher's pulpit directly above it.

N*

Nathaniel's 'multifarious cares' seem to be of a kind which quite frequently fell to a parish clerk, to judge by Dr Johnson's remark that: 'A Parish Clerk should be a man who is able to make a will or write a letter for anyone in the parish.'

l. 44. *forms*. Draws a map or plan (of the land they had measured).

l. 52. *allowance*. Permission.

l. 63. *Launcelot*. Launcelot Gobbo, Shylock's servant in *The Merchant of Venice* (see Act II, scene ii).

l. 76. *from his club*. The private book-club or reading society was fairly common at the end of the eighteenth century, particularly in the small towns or country districts which were not yet served by circulating libraries. After going the round of the members, the books were put up for auction and bought by individual subscribers.

l. 82. *Jane Shore and Rosamond the Fair*. The stories of Jane Shore, mistress of King Edward IV, and Rosamond Fair, mistress of King Henry II, are both told in ballads included in Percy's *Reliques* (1765). Peter's mother had no doubt bought popular broadsheet versions of these ballads from the pack of a travelling chapman.

l. 83. *frail*. i.e. in their resistance to seduction.

l. 101. *Hickerthrift*. Tom Hickathrift, the hero of an old popular romance, was the son of a labourer in the Isle of Ely before the Norman Conquest. According to the legend he was so strong that he was able to kill a giant with the axle-tree and wheel of a wagon.

l. 109. *Fluxions*. The eighteenth-century name for the Newtonian calculus.

l. 109. *Sections*. Conic sections.

l. 123. *Quarles' Emblems*. *Emblems*, by Francis Quarles, a book of rhymed meditations commenting on verses of the Bible, was first published in 1635, and enjoyed a wide popularity, more for its devotional than for its poetic qualities.

l. 128. *the Monthly Magazine*. In the mid-eighteenth century the more popular magazines were often made up to a large extent of extracts (often 'pirated') from current books, poems and plays. Crabbe is careful to make it clear that he is not referring to the new *Monthly Magazine*, started in 1796 and designed for a more cultivated audience.

l. 132. *Tyburn*. Tyburn Gallows (situated somewhere near the modern Marble Arch) was a famous place of public execution from the end of the twelfth century until 1783, after which date the spectacle was transferred to Newgate.

l. 138. *bulks*. Frameworks or stalls projecting from the front of a shop.

ll. 158-69. The suggestion of Wordsworthian influence (apparent from time to time throughout the whole poem) is particularly noticeable here.

l. 169. *Obscure sublime*. Cf. note on Arabella, line 194.

l. 178-9. *computed*. Estimated. The true distance was evidently greater than the popular estimate.

l. 266. *farmer-bailiff*. The steward who managed the Silford Hall estate.

ll. 296-7. The traditional hour for dinner in the eighteenth century had been 2 p.m., but towards the end of the century fashionable circles began to dine later in the afternoon, at about five or six o'clock. Humbler people, however, kept to the old customs, dining in the middle of the day and supping at about six.

l. 310. *to his adventures*. i.e. to the adventures he encountered in his reading.

l. 333. *Narcissus*. The beautiful youth of classical legend who fell in love with his own reflection in a fountain, thinking it to be the nymph of the place.

l. 393. The painting evidently depicted Joseph resisting the advances of Potiphar's wife (see Genesis, xxxix, 7).

l. 397. *peevish*. Perverse, self-willed. In the seventeenth century the word not infrequently has the sense of 'coy' (applied particularly to a woman who resisted the advances of a suitor).

l. 413. *bounds*. Boundary or border (or perhaps here rather 'territory within but close to the border').

l. 421. *Nature*. To 'follow Nature' had been the golden rule for literature and painting throughout the eighteenth century, but the word itself had a shifting ambiguous meaning. It was not confined to the external appearances of natural objects, nor, on the whole, did it carry any suggestion of that which is original, primitive or untamed, but referred rather to the underlying laws believed to govern the natural universe, including mankind. As far as human beings were concerned, it was felt that their essential nature was to be found in its most fully developed form among the educated members of polite civilised society, and not among the primitive, corrupted or depraved. Rousseau and the Romantic movement had, of course, introduced new connotations, but these do not seem to be reflected in Crabbe's use of the word here.

ll. 428-39. The eighteenth century as a whole was a period in which the English aristocracy used their rapidly increasing wealth to fill their country houses with masterpieces of European painting, particularly those from the Italian and Dutch schools. The painters named here are fairly representative of the great collections formed around this time; for, in addition to Titian, the great sixteenth-century Venetian master, the list includes three seventeenth-century painters (now less highly regarded) whom eighteenth-century taste placed in the very first rank—namely, Guido Reni, the Italian painter of the Bolognese school, Claude Lorraine, the French-born painter of Italian landscape, and Gerard Dow, the Dutch painter, pupil of Rembrandt.

l. 453. *Sir Joshua*. Sir Joshua Reynolds (1723-1792), the leading English portrait painter of his day and the first President of the Royal Academy.

l. 476. *awful*. Awe-inspiring.

l. 487. *maces*. The mace was a stick with a flat square head formerly used in billiards, but now superseded by the cue.

l. 503. *gorged*. Swallowed.

ll. 514-47. There has been preserved an earlier version of *Silford Hall* the ending of which developed, and gave much greater prominence to, the moral lesson implicit in these lines.

l. 558. *Bishop Hatto*. Southey's poem *God's Judgment on a Wicked Bishop* (1799) is based upon the tenth-century legend of Hatto, Archbishop of Mainz. In Southey's version Bishop Hatto, in a time of famine, gathered together a great company of the starving poor in his barn on the pretext of feeding them from his own 'plentiful last year's store'. He then locked them in, set fire to the barn, and burnt them all. As a retribution, he was pursued by an army of ten thousand rats; he took refuge from them in his tower on the Rhine, but they followed him there and devoured him.

l. 586. *hydra.* The many-headed snake of Greek legend whose heads grew again as fast as they were cut off.

l. 586. *chimera.* A fire-breathing monster with a lion's head, goat's body and serpent's tail.

l. 669. *The Caliph Haroun.* Haroun-al-Raschid, Caliph of Bagdad, figures in many of the tales of the Arabian Nights.

Try to determine, as precisely as you can, the poet's attitude towards Peter's reading. In particular, to what extent does he approved or disapprove of the influence it has on the boy?

What differences do you notice between this poem and the other poems in this volume, in respect of language, versification, theme and intention?

GENERAL QUESTIONS

1. It is sometimes said that parody is the most effective form of criticism. The following parody appeared in 1812 in *Rejected Addresses*, a collection of parodies of all the leading poets of the day, written actually by two brothers, H. and J. Smith, but published at first anonymously.

What characteristics of Crabbe are 'taken off' in this parody? To what extent do you consider that it constitutes a fair criticism of Crabbe's poetry?

THE THEATRE

by the Rev. G. C.

Interior of a theatre described.—Pit gradually fills.—The check taker.—Pit full.—The orchestra tuned.—One fiddler rather dilatory.—Is reproved—and repents.—Evolutions of a

playbill.—Its final settlement on the spikes.—The gods taken
to task—and why.—Motley group of play-goers.—Holywell
Street, St Pancras.—Emanuel Jennings binds his son apprentice.—Not in London—and why.—Episode of the hat.

'Tis sweet to view from half past five to six,
Our long wax candles, with short cotton wicks,
Touch'd by the lamplighter's Promethean art,
Start into light and make the lighter start:
To see red Phoebus through the gallery pane
Tinge with his beam the beams of Drury Lane,
While gradual parties fill our widen'd pit,
And gape, and gaze, and wonder, ere they sit.

At first, while vacant seats give choice and ease,
Distant or near, they settle where they please;
But when the multitude contracts the span,
And seats are rare, they settle where they can.

Now the full benches, to late comers, doom
No room for standing, miscall'd *standing room*.
Hark! the check taker moody silence breaks,
And bawling 'Pit full', gives the check he takes;
Yet onward still, the gathering numbers cram,
Contending crowders shout the frequent damn,
And all is bustle, squeeze, row, jabbering, and jam.

See to their desks Apollo's sons repair;
Swift rides the rosin o'er the horses' hair:
In unison their various tones to tune
Murmurs the hautboy, growls the hoarse bassoon;
In soft vibration sighs the whispering lute,
Tang goes the harpsichord, too too the flute.
Brays the loud trumpet, squeaks the fiddle sharp,
Winds the french horn, and twangs the tinkling harp:
Till, like great Jove, the leader, figuring in,
Attunes to order the chaotic din.
Now all seems hush'd—but no, one fiddle will
Give, half ashamed, a tiny flourish still;
Foil'd in his crash, the leader of the clan
Reproves with frowns the dilatory man;
Then on his candlestick thrice taps his bow,

Nods a new signal, and away they go.
      Perchance, while pit and gallery cry, 'hats off',
And aw'd consumption checks his chided cough,
Some giggling daughter of the queen of love
Drops, reft of pin, her play-bill from above;
Like Icarus, while laughing galleries clap,
Soars, ducks, and dives in air, the printed scrap;
But, wiser far than he, combustion fears,
And, as it flies, eludes the chandeliers;
Till sinking gradual, with repeated twirl,
It settles, curling, on a fiddler's curl;
Who from his powder'd pate the intruder strikes,
And, for mere malice, sticks it on the spikes.
      Say, why these Babel strains from Babel tongues?
Who's that calls 'silence' with such leathern lungs?
He who, in quest of quiet, 'silence' hoots
Is apt to make the hubbub he imputes.
      What various swains our motley walls contain!
Fashion from Moorfield, honor from Chick Lane;
Bankers from Paper Buildings here resort,
Bankrupts from Golden Square and Riches Court;
From the Haymarket canting rogues in grain,
Gulls from the Poultry, sots from Water Lane;
The lottery cormorant, the auction shark,
The full price master, and the half price clerk;
Boys who long linger at the gallery door,
With pence twice five, they want but twopence more.
Till some Samaritan the twopence spares,
And sends them jumping up the gallery stairs.
Critics we boast who ne'er their malice baulk,
But talk their minds, we wish they'd mind their talk;
Big wordied bullies who by quarrels live,
Who give the lie, and tell the lie they give;
Jews from St Mary Axe, for jobs so wary,
That for old cloaths they'd even axe St Mary;
And bucks with pockets empty as their pate,
Lax in their gaiters, laxer in their gait,
Who oft, when we our house lock up, carouse

With tippling tipsters in a lock up house.
    Yet here, as elsewhere, chance can joy bestow,
Where scowling Fortune seemed to threaten woe.
    Emanuel Jennings brought his youngest boy
Up as a corn cutter, a safe employ;
In Holywell Street St Pancras he was bred,
(At number twenty seven it is said,)
Facing the plough, and near the Granby's head:
He would have bound him to a shop in town,
But with the premium he could not come down;
Pat was the urchin's name, a red hair'd youth,
Fonder of purl and skittle grounds than truth.
Silence, ye gods! to keep your tongues in awe
The muse shall tell an accident she saw.
    Pat Jennings in the upper gallery sat,
But leaning forward, Jennings lost his hat;
Down from the gallery the beaver flew,
And spurn'd the one to settle in the two.
How shall he act? Pay at the gallery door
Two shillings for what cost when new but four?
Now, while his fears anticipate a thief,
John Mullins whispers, take my handkerchief,
Thank you, cries Pat, but one won't make a line;
Take mine, cried Wilson, and cried Stokes, take mine.
A motley cable soon Pat Jennings ties,
Where Spitals-fields with real India vies,
Like Iris' bow, down darts the painted hue,
Starr'd, striped, and spotted, yellow, red, and blue,
Old calico, torn silk, and muslin new.
George Green below, with palpitating hand,
Loops the last 'kerchief to the beaver's band;
Upsoars the prize; the youth, with joy unfeign'd,
Regain'd the felt, and felt what he regain'd,
While to the applauding galleries grateful Pat
Made a low bow, and touched the ransom'd hat.

(The remaining questions consist of comments upon
Crabbe's poetry by various writers. In each case you should

consider and discuss the validity of the judgment, with close reference to the poems you have read.)

2. 'Can he depict character? Yes, but within limits, and he makes no attempt to depict the varieties of speech; his gentry and his outcastes all express themselves in the same formalised diction.' (E. M. Forster)

3. 'Crabbe's astonishing power . . . of dissecting and disentangling that subtle and complicated tissue of habit, and self-love, and affection, which constitutes human character.' (Jeffrey)

4. 'There is no wing in Crabbe, there is no transport, because . . . there is no music. In all poetry, the very highest as well as the very lowest that is still poetry, there is something which transports, and that something in my view is always the music of the verse, of the words, of the cadence of the rhythm, of the sounds super-added to the meaning.' (G. Saintsbury)

5. 'His art is that of the short-story writer and of this he is a master.' (F. R. Leavis)

6. 'The personality of Crabbe as revealed in his poems is definitely unattractive.' (E. M. Forster)

7. '. . . he knows his own powers, and never aims above his reach.' (Southey)

8. 'Crabbe's verses can in no sense be called poetry . . . nineteen out of twenty of his pictures are mere matter of fact.' (Wordsworth)

'The power of touching readers by downright pictures of homespun griefs and sufferings is one which, to my mind, implies some poetical capacity, and which clearly belongs to Crabbe.' (Sir Leslie Stephen)

9. 'Yet Truth sometimes will lend her noblest fires,
   And decorate the verse herself inspires:
   This fact in Virtue's name let Crabbe attest;
   Though nature's sternest painter, yet the best.'   (Byron)

10. 'Mr Crabbe's Tales . . . turn, one and all, upon the same sort of teasing, helpless, mechanical, unimaginative distress; and though it is not easy to lay them down, you never wish to take them up again.' (Hazlitt)

11. 'Pope in worsted stockings.' (H. and J. Smith)

12. 'The Augustan form, as he adapts it, is perfectly suited to his matter and to his outlook—matter and outlook that have close affinities with Jane Austen, though he has a range and a generous masculine strength that bring out by contrast her spinsterly limitations.' (F. R. Leavis)

SUGGESTIONS FOR FURTHER READING

The fullest edition of Crabbe's *Poems* is that edited in three volumes by Sir Adolphus Ward (Cambridge University Press 1905-7); there is also a single-volume collection (edited by A. J. and R. M. Carlyle) published by the Oxford University Press.

Though inaccurate in minor details, *The Life of George Crabbe*, by his son (reprinted in the World's Classics series), makes particularly engaging and attractive reading; and the inaccuracies have been largely corrected in R. Huchon's *George Crabbe and His Times* (1907), a book which does not, however, show much critical perception in relation to Crabbe's poetry.

There is unfortunately very little worthwhile criticism of Crabbe's work, though the reader should not miss the excellent few pages in F. R. Leavis' *Revaluation* (1936). Lilian Haddakin's *The Poetry of Crabbe* (1955) is a useful critical study which should certainly be in the school library. Volume II of Sir Leslie Stephen's *Hours in a Library* contains an interesting though somewhat slight essay, while G. Saintsbury in *Essays in English Literature*, Vol. I (1889), gave a useful survey of the decline in Crabbe's reputation during the nineteenth century. *George Crabbe and Peter Grimes* in E. M. Forster's *Two Cheers for Democracy* is also worth reading.

PRINTED BY
GILMOUR & DEAN LTD
HAMILTON AND LONDON